~~~ **Table of Contents** ~~~

Part 1: Build Your Profile - Choose a topic

To begin your Instagram adventure, the first and most important detail to consider is choosing the right topic for your account. Some people fail to realize that building your account is as important as growing your audience and earning money. They want followers and likes so bad, that they ignore small details like choosing a specific topic or writing a good Instagram biography. If you are one of these types of people and you have no understanding of how the platform works, the best way to start this book is by creating a brand-new Instagram account, regardless of whether you already have one or not. And yes, starting from the beginning can be frustrating because you will have zero followers and no engagement, but at the same time, you will have the power to build your account and see which one of the tips in this book will have the biggest impact on your account. Once you find the right strategy and content for your niche, I guarantee you, you will see your account growing quicker than your previous one. So, when creating a new Instagram account, the first question that should pop up in your head is "How to start?".

And the answer is simple. You need to start by remembering that content creator or not, Instagram is the platform to show the best of your work and using high-quality, eye-catching pictures is the only way to achieve your goals. Wrong or right, this is what people like to see. So, if you are seeking rapid growth, quality content is the first thing you need. And if you want to succeed and grow your fan base, you MUST give 110% of yourself and put every bonus effort and time to constantly improving your profile.

Take it step by step

The first step to consider is choosing a topic, a frame for your account, which can be used as guidance for the rare moment when you run out of ideas and you find yourself searching for inspiration. It is in your hand to choose what you want to achieve with your account and select a topic and a niche for your profile.

If you are still unsure, confused and can't decide on a topic that is suitable for you, there are many options to choose from. Even though there are millions of Instagram profiles, they can be categorized to make it even easier for you to choose a topic that you can relate to.

Note: It is important to post about something you love, and you are passionate about.

There are people with special talents – artists and content creators. Their posts vary between photography, dancing and singing skills, art, fashion and more. If talent is not your thing, there are other ways to keep your profile unique and creative. For example, there are the people, who design their Instagram profiles according to their feed – they keep everything in one color scheme, use a grid layout to organize their posts, the same filters or circle images instead of the traditional square.

Some people prefer to cut one picture into 3, 6 or 9 pieces (which can be annoying). There are also the people who are used as inspiration because of their lifestyle – fitness / yoga gurus, makeup artists, bloggers, nowadays even hairdressers.

But nothing is as big as the category of personal profiles. There are two types of personal profiles. The first type is the profiles that your family members and friends have, sharing their everyday life with the closest range of people, without any desire to grow. The second type of personal profiles is the one wanting to brand themselves because of their work or hobby. This book will focus on the second type, so any time the term "personal profile" is used, you will know that it is about self-branding.

Keep in mind that it is hard to grow your personal profile, displaying your product/ art, because of this huge sea of competition. Plus, it is extremely hard to get noticed when representing yourself. Yes, your personal content might be interesting for your relatives and your group of close friends, but, for the unfamiliar to you user, it is irrelevant and not a good enough reason to hit the follow button because for the people on the Internet, you are just that -

a stranger. If you want to brand yourself, find clients or sell your art, this book will help you convert these strangers into your followers.

Of course, there is one more category – brands. Their topic is clear – to spread the message and beliefs of their company the best way possible through Social Media. And if they do it right, the reward is sweet – bigger brand awareness, an audience of targeted people and a sure increase in revenue. You need to determine the type of your account based on your biggest passion. After all, you will have to stick with the same topic, so choose something you won't get tired of.

Here are some grid styles Instagram accounts can use for their feed:

Tile Grid Composition:

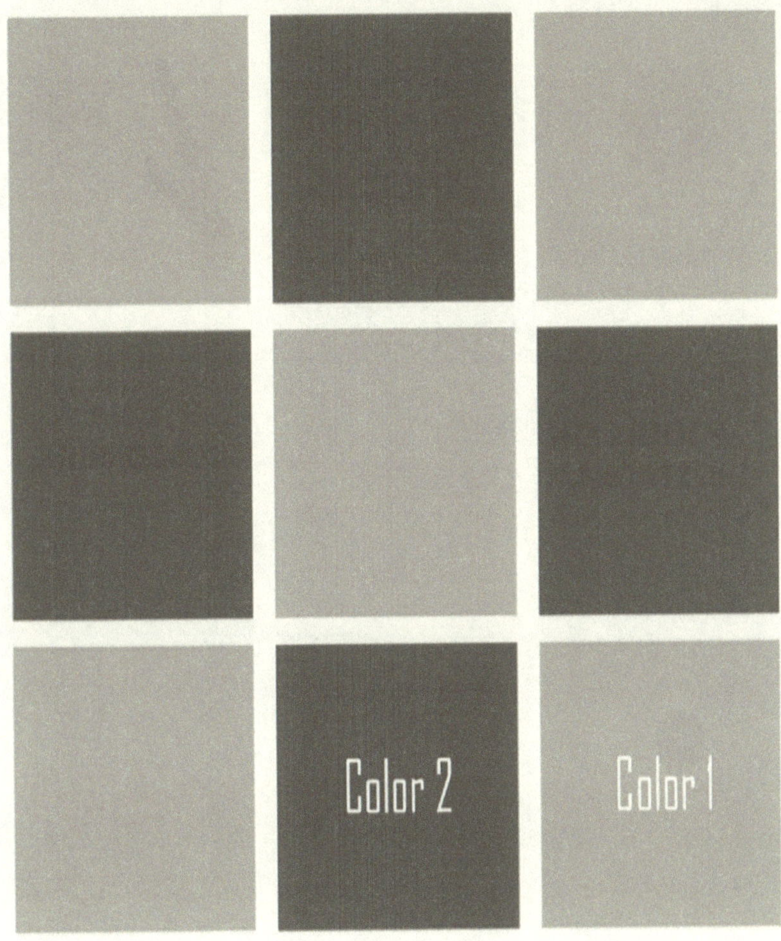

Tile Grid Example:

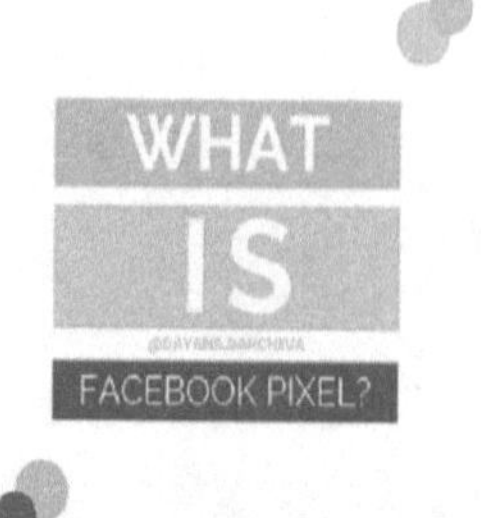

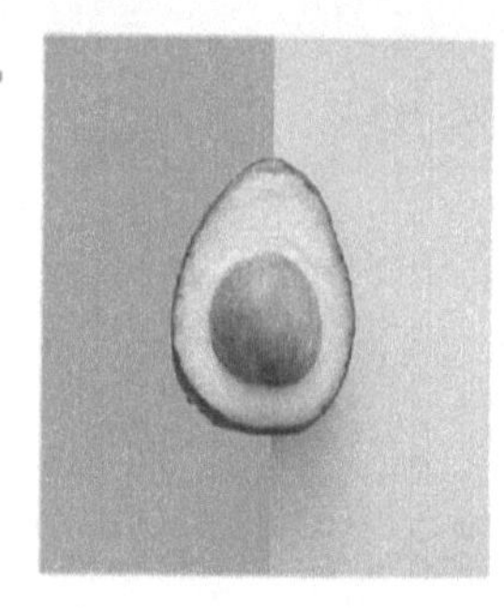

Row-by-row Grid Composition:

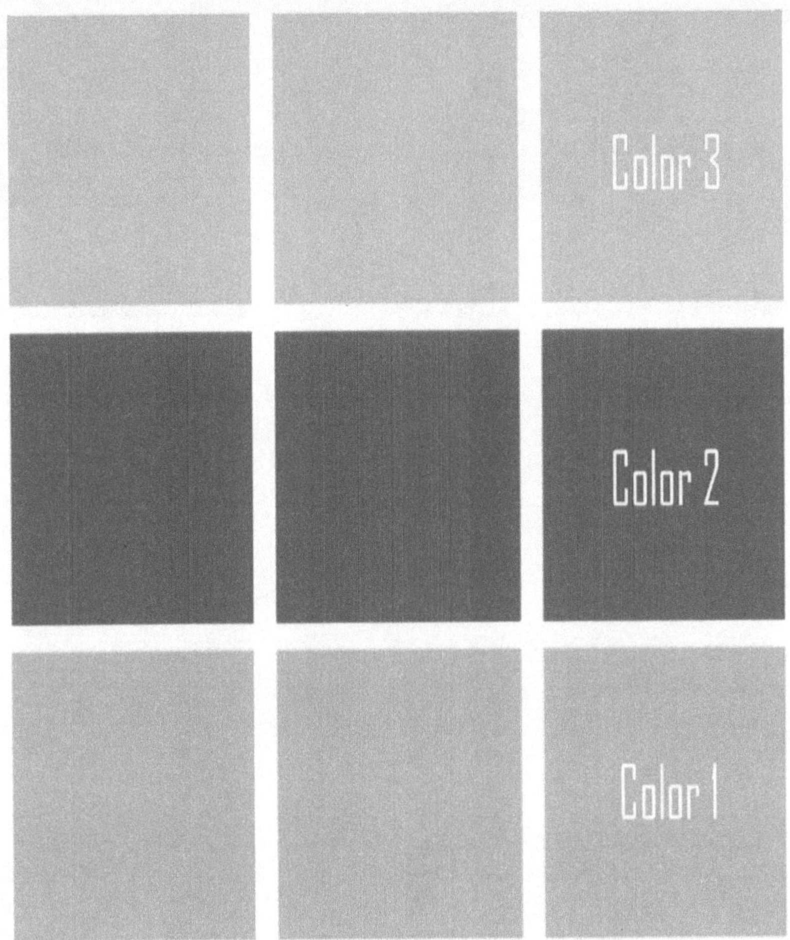

Row-by-row Grid Example:

It feels good to be
lost in the right
direction

Life is either a
daring adventure or
nothing at all

Make each day a
new horizon.

- Helen Keller

Rainbow Grid Composition:

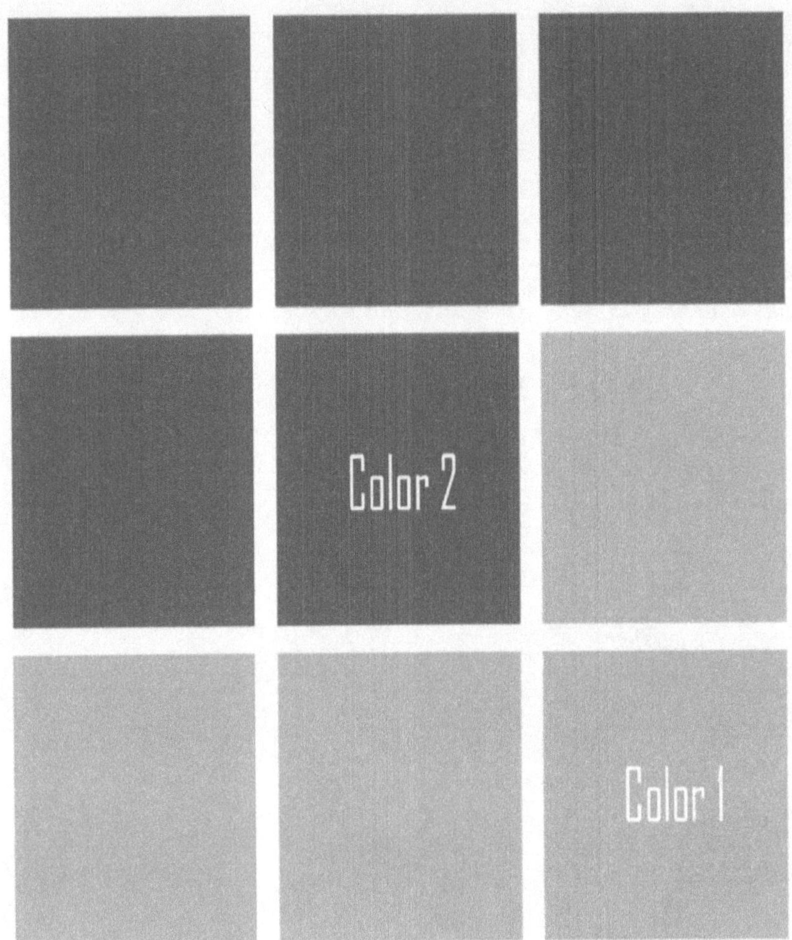

Rainbow Grid Example:

2-1-2 Grid Composition:

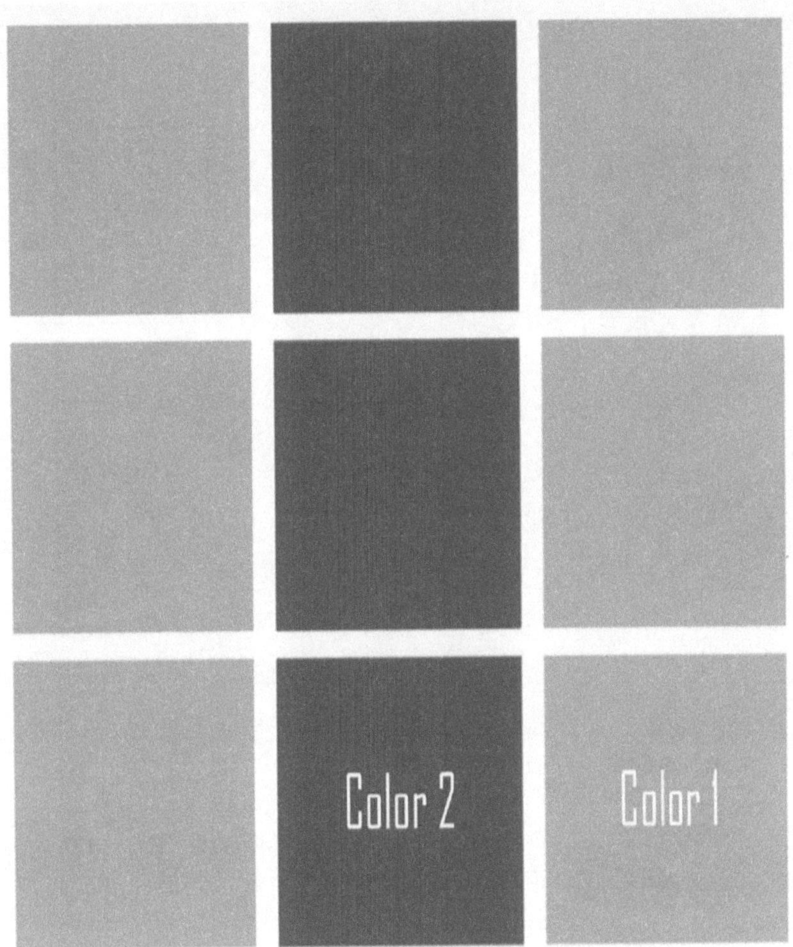

2-1-2 Grid Example:

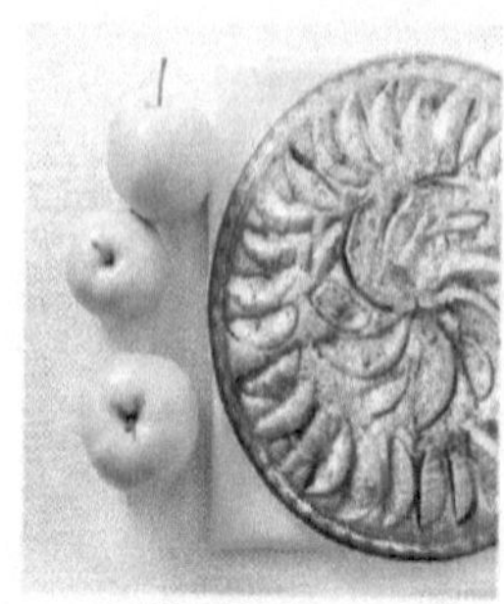

Diagonal Grid Composition:

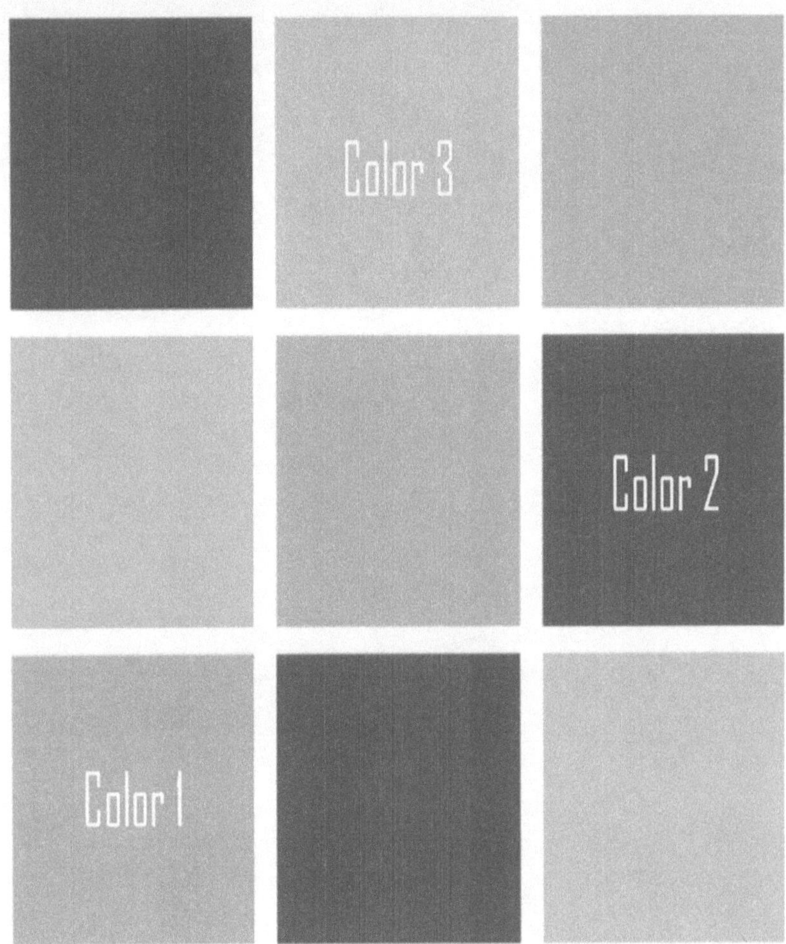

Diagonal Grid Example:

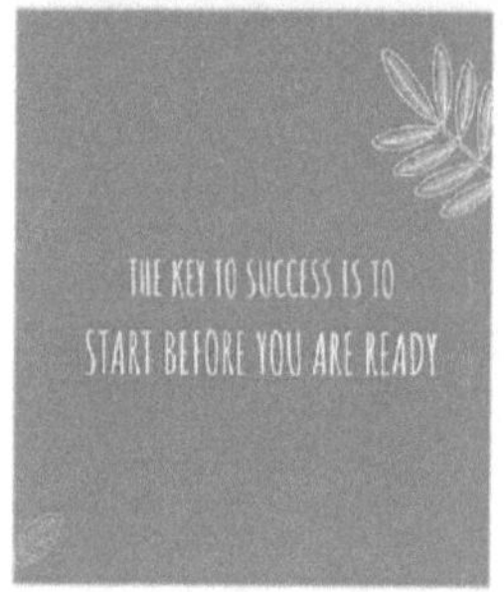  

Creative Instagram Grids Example: Minimalistic

Creative Instagram Grids Example: Circles

Tile Grid Composition. Tile Grid Composition is a mix between two different colors/styles. Brands & personal profiles can use this grid to mix their own content with inspirational messages which makes it an easy option to keep a clean & consistent Instagram feed.

Row-by-Row Grid Composition. Row-by-Row Grid Composition focuses on styling each row (3 posts = 1 row) of your Instagram feed differently. Relatively easy to follow, you can use this style to share quotes, tell a story or share multiple photos with the same background.

Rainbow Grid Composition. Rainbow Grid Composition follows the color of the rainbow. Maintaining such a feed requires a lot of creativity and personality but it can be used by both brands and influencers.

2-1-2 Grid Composition. 2-1-2 Grid Composition is another example of mixing two different colors/styles into one Instagram feed. It looks nice and it is also relatively easy to keep consistent.

Diagonal Grid Composition. Diagonal Grid Composition is a combination between three different colors that you can use to make your Instagram feed more visually appealing. If you are up for a challenge, this style can be the one for you.

Creative Grid Composition. If you have anything else in mind, you can be the one creating your own style of Instagram feed. Just make sure to establish and follow a pattern.

TASKS TO DO:

1. Create a fresh and new Instagram profile.
2. Do some research and look at profiles similar to what you want to achieve with your Instagram.
3. Choose a topic of your Instagram profile.

Part 1: Build Your Profile - Write a good biography

Once you have chosen your topic and niche, it might not be the best time to post your first picture just yet. Instead, focus on adding a meaningful description about your account - write a kick-ass Instagram biography. Well-structured and clean biography always stands out, by making a good impression to every visitor of your profile. Believe it or not, it's a common habit when looking at someone's profile, to look at their brief description about themselves. So, take your time and fill this very important blank place.

You will be surprised how many of the Instagram profiles have empty or unhelpful information about who they are and what they do. This could be a threat to your growth, as you never know when a potential sponsor/client will look at your profile. A weak biography can be crucial, leaving a bad impression you don't need!

How to write your biography?

The best way to write your biography is to look at your profile as a third person - sponsor/customer. This process can help you find the right words and look at the bigger picture. Keep in mind that your space is limited to 150 characters and you need to focus on the most important and exciting information that gives you advantage and makes your account different from the rest of the profiles in the same category. If no ideas pop-up, think about your future content and the topic you have just chosen. For example, travelers, who are going to have their Instagram feed full of new, nice places will eventually symbolize with a world, plane or flag emoticon, or they might mention it in a different form like to symbolize the places they have visited.

Another might prefer to add a sentimental quote that relates to them. Third could reveal personal information about their life.

Using emojis (keep in mind that everything, used in a bigger portion is not good) will give you a better visual and add color to your biography, a statement or inspiration quote will help the people to understand and relate to you and what you stand for, and the personal information could reveal a key detail, that cannot be obtained anywhere else in your profile.

Note: In 2019, Instagram introduced shorter bios. This update cut in half your biography information with the button "more" hiding the rest. Because of this recent change, you will now want to make sure that the first two lines of text in your biography describe and explain exactly who you are. Adding a compelling Call-To-Action after is never a bad idea. This will ensure that you are still getting your message across!

TASKS TO DO:

1. Write down the keywords that describe you best.
2. Create this kick-ass biography description.

Part 1: Build Your Profile - Choose a good profile picture

The profile picture you upload, must be special and memorable. You can still be goofy, serious or crazy. But when it comes to taking the best shot for your Instagram profile, there are some tips and tricks (more like common sense) that you need to be aware of. Let's go through each one of them.

Make it recognizable!

When choosing the best snap for your profile, make sure that the picture is easy to remember. After all, you want to make a good impression and make sure that at least some of your followers will remember your picture and associate it with your profile. Plus, you will need a good one if you are using Instagram stories because your profile picture is the one your followers will see, when you add a story. Your picture combined with the Instagram stories, is a smart trick to outstand the rest of the accounts with stories and make your group of followers remember your account. That way, when you post something new, someone may recognize you, since they have seen the exact same profile picture having a story a few days ago. So, when creating this important element of your Instagram profile, you can experiment, but keep in mind that you must take a high-quality photo and try to make it as unique as possible.

Choose a close-up view!

Second – position your profile picture by focusing on your face. There are many people, who upload full-body look pictures while the face is barely seen. The photo can be gorgeous because of the dress/suit you are wearing on it and might be even the best outfit you own, but consider saving it for a post instead of your profile picture. It is unnecessary to add a picture that compliments your body, considering the small amount of space you are given and the fact that the pictures cannot be zoomed. In the end, your profile picture will look silly. That's why a close-up (face) view is much better. And this works perfectly, but there are some exceptions. For example, when people decide to place a nearly unrecognizable picture with a ton of editing (and blurring their faces, whitening their teeth, etc.) or if they are using one of these crazy animal effects like Snapchat/Instagram filters. Both of them are a big "NO", because it looks childish and not professional. If the goal of your account is to land your first sponsorship, then you will need to make your profile picture to match what you are after.

Ask someone to take the picture instead!

Another great idea to get a good profile picture is by asking a friend to take a few shots of you. Not that selfies are bad, after all, you and only you know best how to pose and what is the best angle for your face. But the front camera of your phone won't take the good quality picture you need. Professional cameras (DSLRs) are the best choice, because they can catch the moment, but don't feel bad if you don't have one. Instead, try to find the best light for your picture, use the back camera of your phone and a friend, who would take the best shots of you.

Keep it memorable but up to date!

Do not stay with the same picture for more than 7-8 months. Try to change and refresh your account once in a while. Don't be the type of person who uses the same profile picture for years. Especially, if your appearance (like the color of your hair, hairstyle or even if you have grown a beard) has changed and it is visible on your recent posts. But don't be the type of people who constantly update their pictures either, because it will get annoying to your followers and you will quickly become unmemorable and not that interesting. Use your Instagram feed to keep the interest of your audience, not your profile picture.

Choosing a profile picture for a business Instagram account is probably the easiest thing. The best profile picture for brands is their logo because this is what you want people to remember. It is a very rare case to see something other than a brand's logo.

Example of Profile pictures (personal profiles):

Personal Profiles

Profile Picture 1
Close-up & Bright colors

Profile Picture 2
Close-up w/accessory

Profile Picture 3
Close-up w/nature

TASKS TO DO:

1. Find the best place & lighting for your picture
2. Take a very good close profile photo

To summarize, if you want to get the most of your Instagram profile, you must have a specific topic, which is like an everyday story to tell the people (your future audience); clean, informative and well-structured biography; a close-up profile picture, easy to remember. These are some of the most important components of building an Instagram account, that people tend to forget or rather ignore.

Take a day or two to focus on these three, so when you start growing, more and more people will be able to get to know you and what you do.

And make sure to choose a topic that you WILL NOT get tired of. It might not make sense now but you need to know that you will not get sick of the topic you've chosen after one year of posting.

Part 1: Build Your Profile - Time, Frequency & Analytics

Now, you can consider the main part of your Instagram profile set. So far, you must have selected a topic that you are passionate about, written an informative biography description and chosen a close-up profile picture (for personal, self-branding) or logo (for brands and corporations) for your Instagram account. Having done all the above, it is time to focus on your content and posts.

However, before you start posting and learn the key secrets of growing and monetizing your account, it is essential for you to set the formalities of your profile. Such as what is the best time to post on Instagram, how often and how to measure your progress (analytics).

Set time to post

There is no need to search on Google articles about when to post on Instagram, when you can learn this information directly from your account. To identify the best time when most of your followers are active, you will need to have at least 100 followers and switch up to a Professional Instagram account. There, you will have two options to choose from - to set a Business Instagram account or a Creator Instagram account. Both of these will give you the same analytics when it comes to when your followers are most active.

For every Instagram account, posting at the "peak time" (when most of your Instagram followers are most active) is a MUST. This is important because you want to get the most initial engagement which is the likes & comments you receive in the first 1-2 hours on your recent post, specifically the ones from your real followers.

High initial engagement on your post will show Instagram algorithm that your content is valuable, which will increase your account's exposure and visibility. Your post will have a higher chance of getting to the Top posts of your hashtag selection and the Explore page and it can even show up in the newsfeed of some of your followers who might have missed it when it was first posted.

If you have a Professional Instagram account and you have reached 100 followers, you can see when your followers are most active from your profile, Insights → Audience (scroll-down to Followers and Voalá, you are there)

Set frequency

Once you agree on when to post, it is time to set a frequency - how often are you going to post. This is an important step for all of us! The frequency can vary from three posts per day to one post per week.

To post less or to post more? - this is the question I get from a lot of my clients. And here is my answer - it is up to you and how much you can handle. You determine your speed and you control how many posts you can create without burning out and running out of ideas.

If you post less content (once a week), let's say once a week, your posts will have time to circulate around Instagram. So even if your post is not seen by the majority of your followers at first, if the Instagram algorithm thinks this is what your followers want to see, your post might end up on your followers' feed later on.

If you post less content, you will have a better engagement rate. When you post daily, you will find it hard to keep the same balance and some of your posts will be more liked than others and vice versa. But if you post less, your most recent post will have time to get likes before the next one comes.

However, if you post less content, make sure to compensate. Keep your accounts active with Instagram stories every single day to make sure your current and potential followers know you are active. You don't need to follow a deadline to post a photo as long as your audience knows you are there.

If you post more content, you will gain followers faster. Although it may sound risky, the more posts you share, the bigger the chance to attract new followers to your profile. If you post more often and use different hashtags, locations, post stories and so on, you will increase your accounts' reach and discovery. The more people see your posts, the more your followers will engage with your content and find it. And even though you are attracting more followers, your account's engagement rate might suffer.

It is up to you to decide if you want to post daily or once a week. Each choice has its advantages. If you post more you will have more followers and grow quickly. While if you post less you will have a better engagement rate and your posts will rank better which will give you slow but steady growth over time.

But do not disappear. Instagram requires a lot of work, if you want to start earning money and build a community around your brand. Don't work harder, work smarter. Set a frequency that works for you and your account. Make it compatible with your goals and strategy. Do not overshare and do not disappear. Don't be afraid to ask for help if you can't do it on your own. There are people who specialize in Instagram and will be more than happy to help. But choose wisely, there are people who use harmful ways to get you fast growth.

Switch to Professional account

The last thing you need to do before you start posting content and growing your account is to switch to a Professional account. This will give you access to unique data and help you track your analytics in order to understand your audience, content and profile better.

You can use Instagram Insights to measure how an individual post is performing:

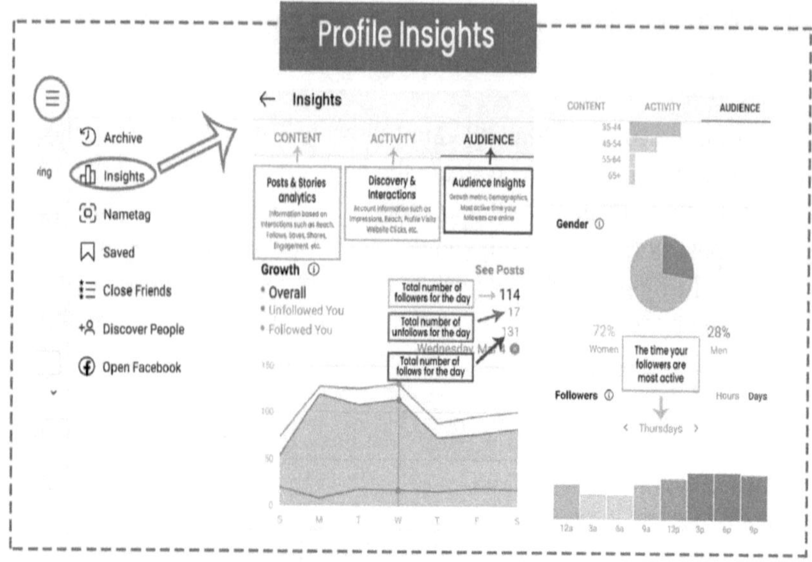
Profile Insights
Archive
Insights
Nametag
Saved
Close Friends
Discover People
Open Facebook
Insights
CONTENT
ACTIVITY
AUDIENCE
Posts & Stories analytics
Information based on Interactions such as Reach, Follows, Saves, Shares, Engagement, etc.
Discovery & Interactions
Account Information such as Impressions, Reach, Profile Visits, Website Clicks, etc.
Audience Insights
Growth metric, Demographics, Most active time your followers are online
Growth
See Posts
Overall
Unfollowed You
Followed You
Total number of followers for the day
114
Total number of unfollows for the day
17
131
Total number of follows for the day
Wednesday, Mar 4
150
100
50
S M T W T F S
CONTENT
ACTIVITY
AUDIENCE
35-44
45-54
55-64
65+
Gender
72%
Women
28%
Men
The time your followers are most active
Followers
Hours Days
Thursdays
12a 3a 6a 9a 12p 3p 6p 9p

Or you can use Instagram Insights to track how your profile is performing:

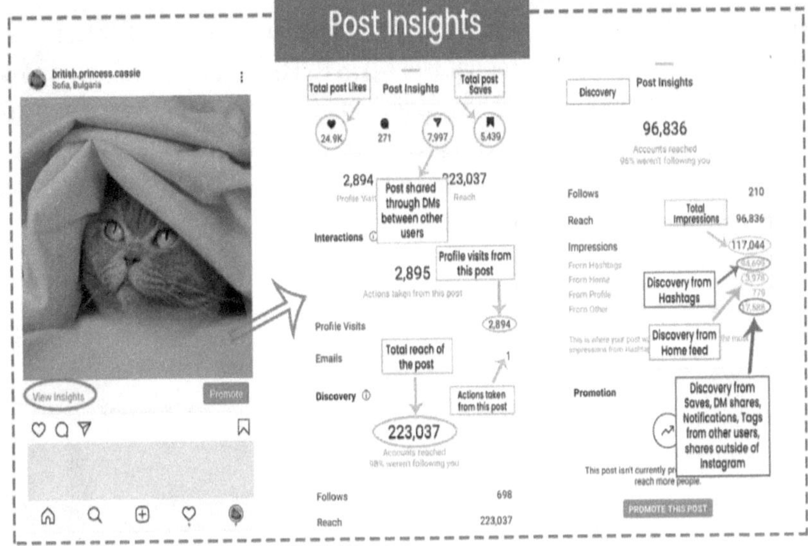

In order to have the option to access Instagram Insights, you will have to connect your Instagram account with a Facebook page. This will also help you with paid advertising later on.

If you would really like to commit to Instagram and what it has to offer, switching to a Professional account is a MUST. To do so, you will need to go to your Instagram profile, open "Settings" and find "Account". Once you are there, you will have to scroll-down until you see a text with blue font. By clicking on this button, you will get to choose between two different account types - a Business or a Creator account.

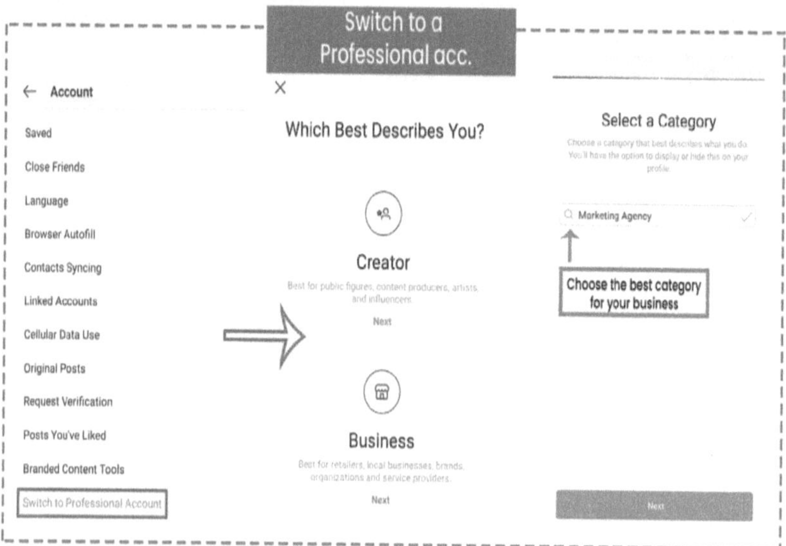

Both of them offer key Insights and access to Facebook Creator Studio. People can use Creator Studio to schedule content in advance from their computers. Creators and businesses can use Creator Studio to prepare content in advance as well as to access their Instagram Insights. Planning & creating content at least one week in advance is a great practice to have everything well planned, organized and avoid experiencing burnout.

Either way, here are the features both options have to offer:

Instagram for Business

Let's start with the Business Instagram account. This is the perfect option for any business owner. If you own a brand - a clothing store, a skincare beauty line, a company in the B2C (Business to Customer) or the B2B (Business to Business) market, this is the obvious choice for you.

What features does it offer?

Instagram Business account was the only available option until 2019. Most of you are probably familiar with it But for those of you who are not, here are the benefits of having a Business account:

- Detailed analytics
- Contact information
- Promotion/Partnership feature
- Quick replies
- Shoppable posts
- Instagram ads

Detailed analytics

With Instagram Business, you get access to a lot of information about your audience (demographics – age, location, when are they active), your content (where did the people come from – is it from hashtags, the Explore page etc.) and your activity (how many people your account has reached for the past week). This is very helpful to know in order to grow your brand. It helps you to get a better understanding of your target audience and content.

You can use Instagram Business to track the performance of your posts and stories. You can see information such as how many of your followers saved your picture and send your post through direct message. You can also see where people are coming from – is it from your hashtag selection, newsfeed or both and much, much more.

Lastly, with the help of the new Growth metric, you can track the number of people who followed or unfollowed your brand every day. This information is very important if you are running an advertising campaign or managing an Influencer campaign because it can show you how your promotional efforts are paying out.

Contact information

With Business account, you will have the ability to add contact buttons directly onto your Instagram profile page. You can add your email, phone number, location and make it easier for your audience to contact you.

Promotion/Partnership feature

This feature is very handy for brands and businesses working with Influencers. The main reason for that is because you are required to disclose sponsored ads if you have any audience from the US or other countries with similar laws. Plus, with the help of this feature, you can track the performance of your sponsored post.

2-tab Inbox

In 2020, Instagram introduced new feature for business accounts – a secondary inbox tab. This new update allows businesses to organize their DMs. with the help of a two-tab system, designed to separate high priority message for low priority ones. With this new feature, business accounts can also sort their DM requests by displaying their 'Top Requests' or 'All Requests'.

Quick replies

If you ever used Direct Messages to communicate with your audience or answer questions to your customers, you probably know how much work and effort goes into answering every single one of the questions. And most of the time, the questions get repetitive.

With Quick Replies, you can create messages that you can later use as answers to commonly asked questions. This feature can be used by every professional Instagram account but especially brands who work with customers on a daily basis. For example, if you frequently get the same question about your shipping costs or the warranty of your products you can set up an answer for each one of these questions.

Then, when the next customer asks you, you can easily insert the previously written message instead of writing a new one. Think of it like a draft message or a note you can always send to whoever needs the information.

Quick replies are great to connect and communicate with your audience. They can be extremely helpful for businesses and marketers. Quick replies are easy to create and can save you a lot of time. So, instead of typing the same long message over and over again, you can save it as a quick message and simply add it to the chat box whenever you need it. But they are available only if you are using the Instagram Business profile.

This feature can be a great addition to your Instagram management. No matter the size of your business, everyone can benefit from using quick replies. Here is how:

It makes teamwork easier. Businesses can set up pre-formatted replies which will ensure that their Social Media channels have a consistent brand voice, even if they are managed by marketing agencies. If an agency is managing the Instagram account of your company, quick replies will make sure that both sides are on the same page.

It helps your brand to develop a certain style & voice. If more than one person is managing the Instagram account of your company, quick replies can be used to stay consistent and keep the same brand voice when communicating with your audience. This will make it nice for the customer, as it will seem like every message is coming from the same person. And that's a nice illusion, isn't it?

Provide Detailed Information. If people are constantly asking the same question and the reply is long and detailed, chances are that you can miss some information when answering it over and over again. Formatting a quick reply in advance will reduce the pressure of answering fast to your customer and give you time to think of every information you need to include in this message.

Excellent Customer Service. DMs can be used to improve your customer service. If your business can provide detailed answers and quick responses to your customers, this would mean you have excellent customer service. Satisfied and happy customers are key to having a profitable brand.

Makes Running Giveaways Easier. There is a lot of fuzz during a giveaway and many people want to know more details than what you've added to the caption of the specific post. For example, people might be curious when the giveaway will end, how will the winner be drawn or will it cost something to collect the reward if the person wins (shipping). So, there is no surprise that some of them would contact you with some additional questions that they would like to know.

Using quick replies will make sure that the company is prepared for the giveaway before it even starts. This will make the process easier when you run the giveaway and start getting very similar questions from different users.

But don't think that quick replies are like chatbots. Their purpose is to help you create meaningful and quality responses, not to make you sound like a robot. Personalize each message and make sure to add a personal touch in each one of them. A simple "Hey Amanda!" at the beginning of the message is better than a cold "Hello!" or no greetings at all.

Shoppable posts

In 2019, Instagram released shoppable posts. One of the best things about this feature is the fact that it does not require a certain amount of followers - any professional Instagram account can have it. And it is a game-changer for every eCommerce business!

With Instagram Shoppable Posts, you have the option to add tags to your posts, show the price of a featured product and visit the website without even leaving the platform. This feature is the perfect tool to increase your sales and bring new customers. For more information about Shoppable post, check out Part 4: Earn money.

Instagram ads

Another option available for both Business and Creator accounts is Instagram advertising. A lot of businesses rely on Instagram advertising because this is a great way to reach your target audience and grow your account faster. More about Instagram advertising, you will see in Part 2: Grow your profile.

Instagram for Creators

Until recently, Instagram Influencers, bloggers, writers, and other creators have had the opportunity to choose between having a business or personal Instagram account, with the obvious choice being the business option. This was the only possibility for entrepreneurs and influencers to get access to features that they can use to understand and grow their accounts. But not anymore.

One major Instagram update released in 2019 is the Instagram Creator account. This new Instagram profile type includes tools and features specifically targeting individuals such as Influencers, public figures, artists, writers, and more. Instagram Creator account is designed for personal profiles who are interested in growing their profile.

Instagram Creator account gives Influencers an alternative option to access analytics and manage their accounts. In fact, Creator account gives people access to a lot of detailed analytics and tools to manage and grow their fanbase.

How to switch to Creator account on Instagram?

If you have been using a business account, you can easily switch up to a Creator account. To do so, go to the option icon in the right upper corner on your Instagram profile page. Then, click on "Settings" and find "Account". Once you are there, you will most likely see the option called "Switch to Creator Account". Click on it, fill the empty fields with relevant information and you will have a Creator account in no time. But keep in mind that switching to a Creator account will make your Instagram account public if it was set to private.

What features does it offer?

If you are interested in switching to an Instagram Creator account, these are the benefits you will receive:

- Detailed Growth Insights
- Direct Messaging Tools
- Flexible labels
- Shoppable posts
- Instagram ads
- Quick replies

Detailed Growth Insights

Similar to the Business account option, with Creator account, you will still have in-depth information about your audience and content. For example, you will still be able to find a lot of information about your posts, stories, account activities as well as learn more about your audience - their age, location, and gender. You can find information about your account performance on your phone, using Instagram Insights or through your computer by using the new feature for creators - Creator Studio. The Instagram Creator Studio gives Influencers daily and weekly insights about their posts, Instagram stories and IGTV account performance. There, you can find all of the important metrics for one Influencer and share them with brand partners.

But the best analytic feature available on Instagram for Professional profiles must be the one that gives creators access to the number of daily follows and unfollows. This metric shows how many followers your account has gained and lost each day and it is updated daily. This new feature can be used by Influencers in their advantage to determine what their audience likes, understand what led to their viral elements vs their worst content and get a feeling what works best for their Instagram account.

Direct Messaging Tools

With the new Creator account comes a filter feature for your DMs (direct messages). This feature is excellent for the ones who get hundreds of DMs because it filters your messages by separating them into three different categories:

Primary: messages that you want to receive and you will be notified of.

General: messages that you don't want notification for.

Requests: messages from people you don't follow.

This feature allows creators to prioritize messages from close ones and have control over their inbox, making follow-up and responding a lot easier. But while it makes DM management easy for creators, it may make it more complicated for brands to reach out.

Quick Tip: If your brand is looking to collaborate with Influencers, it is always a good idea to reach out to them by writing them an email. If email is not an option, try to build a relationship with the Influencer, be genuine and your message will have a bigger chance of being seen. In 2020, Instagram is all about being genuine and stopping bot behavior.

Flexible Labels

Until now, with Instagram Business, you had a CTA (Call-To-Action) option for people visiting your Instagram profile to contact you, using the contact information you have provided. Now, with Creator account, you will have the option to hide your contact information and avoid getting flooded with emails and spam every day. This new feature gives the user more control over who has access to their personal information and who can contact them.

Shoppable posts

Shoppable posts is a new Instagram feature that allows creators to tag brand products and make sales directly from their own Instagram account without leaving the app. This new feature can be very helpful for everyone looking to drive more sales. Including Influencers.

With shoppable posts, Influencers have the opportunity to share shopping information about featured products of their posts with their Instagram audience. This feature gives creators the ability to tag products in their posts, making it easy for their followers to shop their favorite products without even leaving Instagram.

For now, these are the features available for Instagram Creator account but it is almost certain that Instagram will add more and more tools that creators (and businesses) can use to scale and grow their accounts.

And now you know everything there is about Creator account. The question remains:

Instagram Creator vs Instagram Business - which one is better?

Both options have similar features and are almost alike. With Creator account you can still access the same Insights as a Business profile but some options will not be available. For example, if you are using a Creator account, you will not be able to add products from your Facebook page products catalogue (you can still tag products).

Direct Messages will also look different on a Creator compared to a Business account because of the new three categories mentioned above. However, Instagram Creator account is catered to the content creators. Bigger accounts on the platform can use features such as flexible labels and shoppable posts while smaller profiles can take full advantage of Instagram Insights & Post Insights.

TASKS TO DO:

1. Set time and frequency of your posts.
2. Switch to a Professional account (Business / Creator)

Are you ready for the bonus content?

Bonus

Dos & Don'ts

Great job on finishing the first part of the book!

Before we move on with the more complicated part of Instagram, here is a little bonus of Dos and Don'ts on Instagram!

Don't: Be negative!

It is hard to agree with everyone, but if your opinion does not match someone else's don't get in each other's way. If you do, know that sharing your opinion is fine, disrespecting is not. Do not spread negativism and hate but always share your opinion if you feel that it can make a change. Do not hate on your followers and try to do the opposite. Engage with them and try to convert an awkward situation into a nice discussion. If not, move on with your life and pay no attention to the Internet trolls. Plus, if someone is behaving badly, you can always block him. If someone's content is annoying you but you still have an interest in following him, mute the account. This is the friendliest way to do it! If you do not want to associate with a certain individual, you can also remove it from your followers.

Do: Be active on Social Media!

It is hard to be active on Social media when you are living a rushed life. School, jobs, universities, and kids can be very time-consuming and content can be overwhelming, but you can show dedication to your followers by adding or resharing Instagram stories at least once a day. This is just another way to keep your engagement solid and your Instagram feed - clean. Remember to focus on quality, not quantity.

Don't: Lock your profile! / Set it to private!

Many people want to grow their engagement, but at the same time, they are afraid to be seen by "strangers" on the Internet. And I understand that. But if you want more followers and you are taking this road, you should consider making your Instagram profile public.

And don't be mistaken! If you see people with thousands of followers with locked profiles, a lot of the time they have bought their followers likes and comments, or they have made the followers first and something led to locking their account.

Do: Post high-quality content!

Inspire with quotes, tell a story, share hilarious pictures and videos. If you have a pet, let it be the eye-candy of your account. You don't need to fake a luxurious life. But you need to show the best of yours. And this is the mentality you need to have. Check what people like the most out of your feed. And double it. But don't multiply it any further. This is a great strategy! All you need to do is divide your post to a. high engagement and b. regular post, so you can keep the interest in your profile.

Don't: Get Shadowbanned

Even though Instagram hasn't openly admitted it, shadowban has been something, experienced by many in the Instagram community. It is the process of blocking a user's content without the user actually knowing that it is happening. If your account is shadowbanned on Instagram, the content you share won't appear on anyone's feed unless they already follow you.

Shadowbanning addresses the accounts on Instagram that break the rules in an attempt to get more followers and engagement. This process can occur if:

- You are using or have used bots or other automated services, not approved by Instagram TOS (Terms of Use).
- You have used broken hashtags - very popular hashtag who are limited by Instagram because due to having inappropriate content

- You are being a spammer - liking, commenting and following others too quickly.

If you suspect you have been shadowbanned by Instagram, it is fixable:

- Stop using third-party tools to grow your account that violates Instagram's terms of service
- Remove hashtags who might be shadowbanned from your post(s) (you can find a list with shadowbanned hashtags online)
- Delete content that can be perceived as spam or get flagged by others.
- Report your shadowban to Instagram, if you believe your account has nothing to do with any of the above.
- Take a short Instagram break and come back after a few days.

But most importantly - FOLLOW Instagram TOS. Although this won't revive and improve your past content, it will help you avoid getting shadowbanned ever again.

Do: Use Pin Comment

In 2020, Instagram released a new feature to combat negative comments - pin comments. Brands and personal profiles can use this new feature to put comments at the top of their Instagram comments section and focus on positive messages. Instagram users can use pin comments to pin testimonials, positive opinions, answer FAQs, combat misinformation or to start a new conversation with their community.

And while we are still at it …

Don't: Share everything

Do: Master the art of editing your pictures without making them unrecognizable

Don't: Be boring by sticking to only one pose and facial expression

Do: Change locations

Don't: Stick to the same type of content

Do: Share a Throwback photo.

Part 2: Grow your profile

This part of the book will focus on the different ways to grow your account and increase your followers & user engagement. I like to separate them into two categories – harmful and beneficial methods to grow your Instagram. First, I will focus on the top three harmful tricks you need to avoid when growing your Instagram. Then, I will get to the best tactics you can use to effectively grow your profile.

But before I get into this part of the book, know this - I am not here to advise you to buy followers or cheat in any way. It is the opposite. I want to talk about these harmful methods, so you can see that the number of your followers is just that – a number.

So, before I start, I want to answer one question that you probably asked yourself when you stumble upon an account with no good content but with more than 100k/200k/500k followers - What is the secret?

There are people who know how to market themselves and their work. And this is what they do, they focus on content and spend time building a community and forming relationships. They are passionate about their work and they value the offer Social Media gives them. But this is not the case for the people who try to cheat the algorithm.

These are the people - agencies and 'influencers' (not all, of course) who use harmful tricks to rapidly grow their profiles. Tricks such as creating multiple fan pages of the said influencer and linking their real profile in the biography description. So when someone new gets to one of these stan pages, he might think "Oh, this person is someone. Perhaps, I should follow them.".

Or using automated systems (BOTS) to make their Instagram accounts appear less empty. It goes as far as people setting up bots that engage with similar accounts in the specific niche. They work in such a way that they will engage, follow, unfollow, random people and targeted people (like the audience of your competition).

Unfortunately for these users, bots are easy to find and are relatively cheap. And there are so many different bot services available on the market, there should be a demand for such services. But they are not worth it. You will find it more helpful to invest your time and money to create a community that is willing to support you rather than alluring your fans with something fake:

User engagement > Number of followers

With that being said, let's get into part 2 – How to grow your Instagram account?

Part 2: Grow your profile - PODs

(Engagement groups)

Ever since Instagram updated its algorithm to be based on your interests and accounts you often interact with rather than using the chronological feed, PODS appeared. PODs or engagement groups, are one of the most famous methods among influencers to get higher engagement, followers and improve the engagement rate of their accounts in no time. They are private groups of Instagrammers (usually between 10 -15 people), in a similar niche (fashion bloggers, artists, etc.), that have one thing in common - a desire to increase their engagement and outsmart the algorithm. It all happens in the Instagram DMs (short for Direct Messages).

Nowadays, it is harder to find a POD that will freely accept you, but if you are determined you will join one soon or later (you can search through Facebook groups and other Social Media platforms). Each group has its own rules, but they are similar in the way they function - every time you post, you announce it to this closed group of people and they like and comment on your picture. The comments are usually genuine, with the exact topic of the picture. The issue with that is the fact that you have to do the same in return. It is very similar to "like for like" and "comment for comment", but you are doing it with the same people which are also a small part of your followers. And there is a very big chance that Instagram likes your account and pushes your content more, because you are getting great engagement from your followers. The faster the people from the POD like your recent post, the more likeable you will be to Instagram. The platform loves having a high initial engagement (engagement done in the first hour of the post), as it indicates that your account is posting good, high-quality content. And if you are lucky, you will even have the chance to get on the Explore page and get viral or increase your current followers.

People use and like PODs because these groups give them the opportunity to meet new creative people, in the same niche as theirs, from all over the world. But these groups are not all shiny and good. Here is why:

1. It requires A LOT OF WORK. Imagine if you are in a group of 15 people, who post multiple times a day - it can be 3 times, but it can be 5 times. This requires you to write unique and good comments for at least 45 posts per day. This can get very annoying and frustrating.

2. It is FAKE. PODS will most likely give you fake confidence. But the members of the group won't magically buy the product you are offering. In fact, as soon as you stop engaging with them, they will stop engaging with you. Remember, they are there for the same reason as you - to get more engagement.

3. It can and will HURT your brand. Not all of the PODS have these high-quality content and good pictures. And leaving comments on low-quality content every day is not going to look good for your Instagram account.

These are only some of the reasons why PODS are not good for your account. Instagram are aware of the use of PODS and it is a matter of time for them to act and reduce the use of this method. There is a very small chance for them to disappear, as there are other ways to form groups through Viber, WhatsApp, the app Telegram etc. But tricking the algorithm is not good, especially when you can invest the same amount of time (even less) in growing your account the proper way.

Part 2: Grow your profile - Buying FAKE followers

One of the most harmful methods to use when growing your Instagram account is buying fake followers. And because this method is so popular nowadays, it is no wonder that more and more people decide to get on board with it. Many people use fake followers as a base and proof that there is a lot of interest in their profile, fooling other people to hit their follow button. This is done with the intention to get more conversions such as leads and sales. While the rest of Instagram users just want to have more followers. And this is understandable but fake followers are not the way to go and grow.

Why is buying fake followers a bad idea?

Fake followers are not real people. They are bots which on the Internet/Social Media era is equal to a blank number. And the more fake followers you purchase, the more you mess up with your Instagram accounts' engagement rate. And this metric is by far one of the most important for the Instagram algorithm.

So what does engagement rate have to do with buying fake followers?

Because you are buying bots, they won't interact with your profile in any way. Yes, they will follow you but that's all you will get. And for Instagram algorithm, it is important that you get real and organic likes, comments, saves and reshares (through DMs) from the people that follow you or find your profile through hashtags or Explore page.

So you can see how purchasing thousands of followers can hurt your Instagram profile for a long period of time. The more followers you buy (2k,5k,10k,50k) the harder it will be to get your account back on the right track. Some people will try to keep the "fake effect" on for as long as they can. They will even go one step further and purchase likes & comments for their posts, so you can never tell if it is fake or not. However, Instagram is pretty strict when it comes to bots, so soon or later you will be caught and you might lose the money you have invested in your account and get banned. In addition, if you get caught with fake followers, this will hurt your credibility in front of your real audience. Fake followers are against the Instagram Terms of Use, so if you are okay with having a chance to shut down your account and lose your money and progress, you can go for it.

Plus, by buying fake followers, you lose the real social element. As a brand or a personal profile, you want to listen to your target group and pay close attention to what they really want to see from your profile. So, when your next product or video/article launches, you can deliver to your audience what they've wanted. Feedback is very important for growth and it is something that fake followers won't give you.

Building your account comes with growing a stable community. The numbers are important, but you need to stay true to yourself. In the world of Social Media, people shouldn't care about the number of their followers, but finding the right niche and building relationships with the people interested in their product/service/persona. Engaging with your audience and making story polls can help you define the market better and give your followers what they want. Having a Social Media Strategy and clear goals will help you to reach out to your target group, better and faster than any bot.

While if you buy bots and your followers are unable to engage in any way with your content, this will decrease your engagement rate. In fact, if you buy hundreds of thousands of followers your engagement rate might get to a point where it is irreversibly bad and you will have to create a new Instagram account and start over again.

Part 2: Grow your profile - Follow/Unfollow

If you haven't heard of buying followers or the follow/unfollow trick, you must be new to Instagram. The idea behind follow/unfollow is to follow someone and hope that the person will notice your profile and follow you back because they got a notification with your name. After a couple of days (1 – 3) pass, you unfollow them regardless of their actions. That way some of them might forget that they are following you or like your account, so much that they become your real followers, even if you are not following them back.

There are two types of people who follow/unfollow. The first type is the people, who want to grow faster and they don't have time to do it organically. Usually, they follow and unfollow accounts using a third - party application, where they can see who unfollowed them. They are the same people who use the #spam4spam or create "gain trains" (tagging people, so you can easily find your next person to follow; some gain trains require users to follow a specific number of the people commenting on their posts).

The rest use bots and spam accounts. Because these services are automated, the bot will like, comment and follow/unfollow accounts, based on the specific accounts you've selected (usually the biggest accounts in your niche). It will do the work while you are sleeping, eating and working.

Follow/unfollow has been known for years and there are mixed opinions about it. Some are happy with the result, others think it is not their thing. Unfortunately, more and more companies and personal profiles use this method because they want to grow immediately. It is one of the few ways to see instant progress and to get hundreds of followers in a short period of time.

If you want to be a part of this fake show, know one thing - this trick is very time consuming, but it is nothing compared to the spammy, poor-quality posts that your Instagram newsfeed will get. That's not all. Using the follow/unfollow technique discourages smaller bloggers, influencers and brands. Not being able to keep the same number of followers, or even worse - losing followers because of people using this method is very discouraging for someone, who is just starting out and is dedicated to their feed and content.

It is hard to know whether one brand has a loyal group of people as part of its followers, but know this - an account with 800 dedicated followers can make at least a few sales and get a small group of loyal followers. While an account built using "follow for follow" won't. Most of the people who follow/unfollow don't care who you are or what you are selling, they don't even care about your content.

Using this strategy to grow is definitely not for everyone, but for those of you who want to give it a try, know that this can hurt your image and leave your account with a bad engagement rate. Not only that, with follow/ unfollow you will attract a group of people, interested in your follow as a number. Most of them won't even try to connect with what you do or become interested in your products. Similar to buying followers, using this harmful trick will damage your brand and credibility. People will notice if your followers are not on the same level as your engagement. Everyone who is willing to do 2-minute research will see it. From a personal profile perspective, fewer brands will be willing to work with you. While from a brand perspective, you will lose the trust of your followers which can damage your brand's credibility.

Follow/unfollow works because it gives you fast results. With this growth hack, it can take you one week to get to your first 1000 followers. Some of the accounts might even like and leave a comment under your posts. You can climb to 10 000 followers in no time.

But the moment you stop, your profile will start going down. While if you work hard to get to your first 1000 followers, you will see how more and more accounts decide to follow you every day because of the content you create or the personality you have. So, even if you take a break from Instagram for a few days, your followers won't drop, quite the opposite – there is a very high chance that they keep growing. And this is your goal. This is what you want to achieve. This is what I want to help you achieve!

All of these three methods - PODs, fake followers and follow/unfollow - have the same consequences. They are not aligned with Instagram Terms of Use, so there is always the potential chance to get banned or hurt your profile one way or another.

Part 2: Grow your profile - Hashtags

Instagram hashtags are one of the most obvious and efficient ways to grow your account in terms of followers and engagement. And it is not hard to use them. But many people don't feel that way as there are so many examples of people using hashtags poorly. In this chapter, we are going to focus on how to find hashtags for your profile, how many hashtags you need to use and mistakes you need to avoid when choosing the right hashtags.

With the help of hashtags, you can make your content more discoverable by targeting a specific group of people, interested in YOUR niche. Placing your content in front of the people, interested in your topic and getting it all for FREE is what makes hashtags so valuable. Plus, a combination of nice content and catchy captions are nothing without an efficient hashtags strategy. To understand how hashtags work, think of them as short phrases who can help you categorize your content on Instagram. Hashtags will help you increase your engagement - likes, comments, story views, and followers by attracting the right group of people who are most likely interested in what you share on Instagram.

If you are still not convinced that hashtags are a good idea for your

Instagram, did you know that posts with at least one hashtag in it gets about 13% (on average) more engagement than a post without any?

Hashtags are simply a better way to categorize your content (posts). So where does it all go wrong and why are you not getting where you want to be?

Many people don't have a clear goal behind their Instagram account. They don't know what they want to achieve, nor how to achieve it. So, what they do is they add a group of 30 hashtags (generated from an app) and they hope for a miracle. But using a set of hashtags that has been used by MANY other accounts is more like winning the lottery - what are the odds?

Your engagement won't increase that much and if it does, it won't be by its full potential. This is why hashtags are frustrating for so many people and why using them is not beneficial for their businesses. How to fix this?

Each industry has its own niche and challenges to deal with, but when it comes to hashtags rule number one is to don't use the trending one word hashtags (#girl, #fitness, #life, etc.). They are so popular and the competition there is HUGE. The number of hashtags per post is limited and you don't want to waste it on a hashtag that most of the people won't see because of the fast user uploads. Think of it this way – the trending hashtags have a volume of (let's say) 40 million posts, meaning that every second multiple posts (pictures and videos) are added in the recent tab of this specific trending hashtag. This moves your post below and makes it impossible to be found by potential followers. Not only that, one of your goals must be to rank for the Top post, because your picture will be seen by anyone who writes the specific hashtag. If your post gets to the Top post section of 5 of your hashtags, it will stay there for a while (a few hours - two/three days). This is a great opportunity to get more followers and understand which hashtag works for your content. So, you can see how hashtags like #fitness and #food are not suitable for your account, even if you are a fitness trainer or a chef.

Try to use more specific hashtags that don't have millions of posts. For example, if you are posting a picture of your dog, instead of using #dog, try to specify the breed of your pet such as #cockerspaniel. That way, people interested in this dog breed can easily find you by specifying what they are looking for. Forming hashtags from three or four different words such as #dogsoftheday can also fit your picture better than #dog. You don't always need to use smaller-volume hashtags, but it is a great beginning for every new account.

Note: Growing your account requires a lot of patience and involvement. One last thing, the limit of hashtags per post is 30 hashtags and it is good to start with that exact number for each one of your posts. If you can get 30 opportunities to increase your Instagram engagement, why not use the 30 hashtags?

But how to find the right hashtags for your account?

Instagram Algorithm

In order for you to find hashtags and get the most out of your engagement, you will need to keep up with the recent Instagram algorithm. The company updates its algorithm all the time, so you will need to know which update will hurt your strategy and which won't. For example, there are some people using a set of 30 hashtags in the caption and then another 30 in the comments. That tactic used to work, but not anymore. However, some people don't know that this came with one of the Instagram updates, so they keep using the total 60 hashtags. This can be bad if you are a brand, promoting premium products because it doesn't look optimistic and trustworthy in the eyes of your potential customers.

Competition

If you are a new account and you have no clue where to start from, it might be a good idea to take a look at the people in your niche (your competition) and check out what kind of hashtags they are using. Researching the competition can give you some idea about which hashtag can work and which one won't. Brands are not the only one you can research. Influencers (people, with large Social Media following) in your industry can help you understand what people like your niche and give you some extra insights on the group of hashtags they are using.

Find your own

This one is a must, even if you are just starting your Instagram account. The sooner you learn how to find hashtags on your own without wasting a lot of time, the faster you will grow (it still takes a lot of patience).

You can start by analyzing the volume of the hashtags through different websites or the Instagram app. Using a website is more time consuming, because you will have to do double work by searching the hashtags on Instagram and then adding them manually to the website, but there are some pros. For example, websites like Hashtagify.me will show you a lot of information about the specific hashtag, such as Recent Popularity and how trending is the hashtag for the month/week.

If you think this is too much work, Instagram itself is great to discover hashtags. To do so, simply start typing into Instagram's search bar a specific phrase from your niche and you will see related hashtags in the scroll-down menu and their volume. These are great suggestions that you can use to gather as many hashtags as you can.

So how do I find hashtags?

If it is a new account that I have just started working on or my own, I always start by researching the niche - competitions and other accounts with similar content who get a lot of traction.

Next, if suitable, I will also look for accounts willing to give my new Instagram a feature (repost my post on their profile). These are special accounts who curate content on Instagram and are willing to give you a shout out. It is not hard to find features. For example, if you are a painter and you want to boost your Instagram by also attracting the right group of people, you might take a look at the hashtag #artfeature. There, you might find many accounts who do just that. Usually they use their own branded hashtag so they can easily discover and curate new content from the people who want to be featured. However, the problem with features is that not every time you get the boost you have expected.

Then, I research my hashtags by typing # + the beginning of the word I need in the Search section on Instagram. Here is where you get creative and think of stuff that goes well with your niche. For example, if my post is about a cat, I can use all sorts of combination with it - #fluffycat, #lazycat, #catplays, #instacat, etc. This way, you have a great variety of hashtags to choose from.

Typically, I create about 3-5 sets of different hashtags, as using the same hashtags everyday might get annoying for the people, who regularly check or follow them. Plus, using the same hashtags over and over again is not a good sign for Instagram algorithm and your account might get shadowbanned. But if you form a few different sets of hashtags, they will give your account bigger exposure and opportunity to reach a new audience. If you use one set of 30 hashtags in all of your posts, you will have 30 ways for people to find your profile. But if you use 5 different sets on your various posts, you will have 150 ways to have your profile discovered.

However, sometimes it is hard to replace the main hashtags. These are the hashtags who describe your niche and Instagram account the best. They are your core hashtags. For example, if your account is about digital art, it might be best if you use #digitalart in all of your sets. Or if you are a Digital Marketing agency, #digitalmarketingagency is a key hashtag for your account. I try to stick to 2-5 main hashtags and I add them to all of my sets.

Once I have my main hashtags, my technique is to combine hashtags with different volumes. The combination that works for me in general is:

- No more than 5 hashtags within the range of 2M - 10M (million) posts
- 10 - 15 hashtags with the volume between 100 000 - 500 000 posts
- The rest I fill with hashtags that have a much smaller volume such as 50 000 - 100 0000 posts.

I rarely use 30 hashtags - my posts vary between 20 - 26 hashtags, as I find it more efficient.

The second combination I try to work with is using a mix of middle- and small-volumed hashtags. The size of the hashtags in this case varies between 50 000 - 500 000 posts.

The key with Instagram hashtags is to find your own mixture that works for your niche, as some of the industries (for example makeup) are too big compared to others.

There are two types of hashtags - branded and community.

• Branded hashtags are specific to your brand (your company). They can be helpful for both - brands and personal profiles. Branded hashtags can be extremely useful when running a campaign to promote a product or if you are organizing a giveaway. They are also used to increase brand awareness. Remember, a campaign hashtag has to be:

1. Memorable - so more people can use it

2. Align with your brand's message - so people can get to know your brand more

3. Catchy & Engaging - creating unique and catchy hashtags for your followers will help you see how many people are participating and getting hyped for your campaign

• Community hashtags are the general hashtags we all use. It can #ootd or #followme. They are widely used across the platform as they are not tied up to a specific person or company. They are used to build an audience, get discovered and connect with people with similar interests.

Using community hashtags is a MUST, at least when you first start your Instagram account. Once you grow an audience, you can start introducing your own branded hashtags and encourage your followers to use or follow them.

What is the magic number?

There isn't a specific number of hashtags that will guarantee you better results. Many brands use between 5-7 hashtags on each post, so there are a lot of people assuming that this is the magic number. But this is not the case. The number can vary depending on the industry that you are in and how big is your Instagram account. The best way for you to find out is to test and test and test all over again.

But don't settle. NEVER settle! Yes, the group of hashtags might be working at the moment, but there is a very high possibility that people following the hashtags will get bored of seeing your content and ignore it. Plus, changing the hashtags might lead to reaching new people, interested in your content. And we all want that at the end of the day.

Note: If you post more than 30 hashtags, your post will be published without the caption and the hashtags, so make sure to keep a track of the number of hashtags when posting.

How to grow your account using hashtags?

One of the most difficult things is to apply the theory into practice. So, here is some extra Information that will give you an idea of how hashtags can help you grow.

Do it with style. Style your captions the best way possible, so you can make your posts look great and not frustrating and confusing for the newcomers. You can use emojis, empty space or dots to divide your caption from your hashtag. Remember, you can use 30 hashtags and change them every day, but your content, the actual picture/video/GIF is what makes people connect and engage with you.

Use ONLY relevant hashtags. Back in the days (when Instagram first launched), using #fitness was getting you a solid engagement, even if your post had a completely different topic. But with the huge competition there is today, you need to optimize your hashtags by using the most specific hashtags you can and ONLY them. Your posts will perform better and more people will engage with you if you use 26 out of 26 niche hashtags in your industry.

Join trending events that get people excited. There are some rare exceptions where using trending hashtags, not directly connected to your business can be helpful for your account. For example, if the world is excited about the end of GoT or the World Cup. Be creative and try to find a way to connect your industry to the trending event, so it doesn't look fake.

Use less frequently used hashtags. There is no secret that this tactic can bring your account a lot. But before you start using it, be aware that hashtags that are less frequently used are less searched.

Follow your main hashtags. As I have already mentioned, once you choose a niche for your account, you will have a few main hashtags. There, you will find a lot of potential followers and opportunities to build relationships with people in your niche. If you don't want to miss out on good quality content to engage with, you might want to follow your main hashtags.

Note: This will not in any way affect your Instagram following number. When you follow hashtags, it is visible to anyone. To see the hashtags you follow, go to your Instagram profile and click on Following. Then, you will have the option to choose between the people and hashtags you follow.

Add hashtags to your story. Instagram stories have the option to add one hashtag per upload. This is a big "YES" for me and you will later learn why.

Measure the performance of your posts and pay close attention

to the most engaged set of hashtags. Analytics can help you find which post performs better than the others. You can pay close attention to the most engaged set of hashtags if you have a Professional profile. You can find more information about how many people came from hashtags and determine which set is good and which one is bad from Post Insights, under every one of your posts. Plus, if you are lucky, you will have the awesome feature called Hashtag Insights.

Instagram has recently launched the feature we all have been craving for - Hashtag Insights. Although the feature is not available for my account (as for the moment of writing), this feature is a game-changer for everyone. With Hashtag Insights, you are able to easily determine if your Instagram hashtag strategy is working or not.

If you are among the lucky people who have this feature, you can find it in 'View Insights', located under the specific Instagram post. From there, all you need to do is to scroll down until you see the section called 'Impressions from hashtags'. You will see your top hashtag selection as well as how many impressions it brought to your post.

One of the biggest benefits of implementing a hashtag strategy is seeing how your audience grows and the way your community is formed. Building a strong community requires a lot of work and good content.

But hashtags are not everything! Creating an efficient Social Media strategy with clear goals and a room for improvement is the first step to grow your account. So, if you don't utilize the right strategy and don't have clear goals, investing all this time will be pointless and discouraging.

Part 2: Grow your profile - Instagram Stories

By today's date, over 500 million users use Instagram stories every day. Roughly, this is about half of the people who use this platform. Having this many users, has given Instagram stories some really cool features. With stories, you can grow your account and make your audience more engaging at the same time. You can use them to increase your brand awareness or learn more about the preferences of your target group. Or to keep your profile active. Either way, Instagram stories are very important and should be a part of your Social Media strategy. To get started, let's get through all of the stickers available on the app.

Stickers - Hashtags

You can use hashtags to increase your account's visibility and bring unique viewers to your story and profile. There are two ways to add hashtags to your Instagram story. The first one is to open Stickers and choose the hashtag option. Or if you want it to be more customizable, you can also do it from the text field by starting the text with the hashtag (#) symbol.

To use a story hashtag efficiently, you will first have to hit 500 followers. Otherwise you will find it hard to compete with the rest of the Instagram accounts who use the same hashtag and your stories will get no views. So, if you are struggling to get viewers from story hashtags this might be the reason. As well as using too big hashtags for your niche.

Just as the regular hashtags, if you don't use the right ones, you will not get very good results. For example, if you use the tag #cutecat and your story does not feature a cat in any way, you will not get views from this hashtag because Instagram algorithm will most likely find your story irrelevant for this specific hashtag. Instagram is a visual engine, so it is important to categorize your stories with the best suitable hashtag for the occasion.

On Instagram stories, you can use multiple hashtags. However, 1-3 of them will give you significantly better viewer count. The rest might not give you any new viewers. So there is no point in using 5-7-10 hashtags per story. Instead, try to focus on 1-3 hashtags that describe your story best. If your story has a strong message and your Instagram account consists of high quality content, some of these viewers might turn into engaging followers. And as a brand and a personal profile, you would want to have followers who are active on Instagram and will engage with your stories and content.

Stickers - Geotag (location tag)

You can also add a location tag to your Instagram story. The biggest advantage of choosing a location for your story is to attract local people. As a brand, this can be very handy for the people in your area, looking for a service that you are offering because you will get a lot of exposure. Geotag or location tag can help personal profiles too. For example, travel bloggers can use it when visiting different places around the world. Similar to the hashtag sticker, if you have a captivating story and a well-thought out Instagram feed, you won't find it very hard to get some followers from using location tag. Once you start using it, you will see how many new people will view your story and how many of them will follow you. Then, you can determine if this is worth it for your Instagram account.

Stickers - Polls & Quiz

You can also use polls in Instagram stories. With polls, you will have the option to ask a question and create two answers for your followers to select from. This feature can be used as a smart marketing tool to get to know your Instagram audience better. Whether it is about a product you have sold or a blog post that you have created, asking for feedback and using the information that comes directly from your target group can help you learn more about their taste & personal preferences.

If you need more than two answers, you can use the Quiz sticker instead of Polls. This sticker can help you create up to 4 answers, giving your followers more options to choose from.

It is important to give your audience variety. So don't post the same type of content and don't overuse Polls or Quiz. They can get annoying and your account can suffer from losing followers.

Stickers - Ask a Question

You can also encourage your viewers to engage with your account, using the Instagram feature "Ask a Question". As the name suggests with this feature you can ask questions to which your target audience can give answers. And it is up to if you would like to share the answer with your Instagram community. This feature is a great way to give your Instagram more personality. Plus, you can reuse some of your old content to provide meaningful answers to your stories.

Stickers - Countdown

The countdown clock sticker has been recently added to the Instagram story. Brands and personal profiles can use it to create hype around their new announcements, products, promote events, future posts, really anything that comes to the mind. You can set the date and time you want to be counting down to and customize it with other stickers, GIFs, text, emojis.

Stickers - Donate

With this sticker, Instagram gave users the option to raise money for different non-profit groups. The Donation sticker is the perfect feature for charity and non-profit organizations looking to raise money for their cause.

Stickers - Chat

Another great update from Instagram is the launch of the Chat sticker. Because Instagram is all about communicating, this sticker is the missing piece you would want to know about. When users click on the Chat sticker, they can request to join a specific group, and the account holder can approve these requests as they see fit. Although the Chat sticker is a great feature, it can be tricky for the user.

When you use the Chat sticker you would want to make sure you are not exposing the chat group in front of too many eyes. In order to save the value of the group, make sure to include only the right group of people. For example, if you have an exclusive sale, make sure to create a group only for your most loyal followers.

The chat sticker is an interesting feature but it is not a mandatory part of your Social Media Strategy. Unlike the rest stickers like Countdown and Donate, the Chat sticker is not a must and cannot offer too much to brands and personal profiles.

Stickers - Website traffic

If your account has above 10 000 followers and it is a Professional Instagram account, then you can grab the opportunity and add a link to your Instagram story. This is something that you must look forward to. Why?

Many companies are willing to pay a lot of money to get website traffic by promoting content throughout the different Social Media Platforms. But with the help of Instagram stories, you can get free organic traffic to your blog, products, or anything you want to share with your followers. The secret ingredient is to add a clear CTA (Call To Action) message that will encourage your followers to "swipe up" and look at your content. Some great CTA messages are: "See more"; "Join Now"; "Swipe up"; "Visit Today..."

Storytelling

Use your Instagram story to tell one! Yet another great way to keep your engagement and interest in your profile is by creating a story that people would like to follow. To get a better understanding, imagine dividing your story in three different pictures, following the same path. The idea is to add story by story with a few hours difference and add engaging, catchy text, that will attract more eyeballs. Keeping the mystery with creative stories can become something that your followers are looking for. Similar to polls, don't overuse storytelling, as it will get annoying and the level of excitement for your followers will drop. Plus, mixing is the key to staying interesting and relevant.

Stickers - Go LIVE

Do you know what is better than sharing a story - Going LIVE!

Giving your followers a taste of your life might open new opportunities for you and make them even more attached to your profile. This is a great way to get noticed and connect with your audience.

It can also help you climb in front of the other people, sharing a picture or a video to their story. And this is something that you want. Because more interest means staying on the top of your followers' news feed. Being in front of the other stories is great for your brand awareness and creates consistency, because your devoted followers will be reminded of your existence, everytime you add a new story.

Collaborations

One of the most powerful ways to increase your group of followers (not only with Instagram stories) is to collaborate with bloggers and influencers in your niche. Working on a secret project with people, having the same interests as you can turn into a great experience, and build a relationship that your (and their) followers will love. So, if you decide to collaborate with someone from your niche, make sure that you tease your followers through the Instagram stories. You can make people curious by tagging someone on your story. This can be great for their profile as some of your followers might find their account interesting. The best thing about it is that they will return the favor, bringing their followers to your profile. Great right?

Takeover

Another way to connect with influencers in your niche is to do a takeover. Takeover is when another Instagrammer takes your account for a day (24H period) and vice versa. If you are the one taking over the Instagram of someone else, make sure that you have strong content. Prepare an interesting day for the new followers, so that some of them become so impressed with you, that they turn into your followers too.

Takeovers are not as scary and do not necessarily require giving your password and account away. In fact, if you work with people in your location, you can meet and exchange tips & tricks and do the takeover under their supervision. Another way to do that is by scheduling content and sending it to them.

The ideal outcome of a takeover is to attract people to your profile and convert some of them to followers. This is not easy to achieve, but engaging and interacting with the audience during the takeover can help you grow.

Paid advertising

If you want to get the maximum of a Social Media Campaign, Instagram stories paid advertising should be considered as one of the main elements. When promoting a product, it is important to reach the audience you want, YOUR target group. The great news is that you can do it using Instagram stories. Instagram made it easy for teams, as you can send a prototype to your co-workers of how your Instagram story ad would look like. Plus, now you can use stickers for your ads. For example, Instagram users have the option to add a polling question sticker as part of their story ad. This can be a very powerful feature for Marketers if they need to make a survey about a certain product. Of course, this type of promotion involves spending money, so consider using one of the upper tips if you don't have the budget for an ad campaign.

Instagram stories - Create

Creating different stories for your Instagram account will make your audience more engaging. Although we already have so many platforms and apps that offer story templates, Instagram introduced its own story templates in 2019. The new additions contain pre-designed Instagram stories with an option to fill the empty space with your own content. Instagram templates can make the Highlights of your account amazing, informative and different.

In order to use one of the available Instagram stories templates, simply open your Instagram stories camera and swipe left from your home feed that is set to "Normal". Swipe one time in the lower end of your phone screen and you will find "Create". Once you are there, you will have to swipe right until you reach the template section. It starts with text, shoutouts, GIFs and then you will see templates. You can tap on them in order to change the template with the next one in line or you can preview all of them by clicking "See all". When you have found your best design, just tap on the template symbol in the circle below and you will be ready to add final touches and post your story.

With so many available features, you will find it easy to create stories on a regular basis. But if you are left with no options, Instagram has two more features you could benefit from: - "On This Day" and Repost features.

"On this day"

This feature is very similar to what we have seen on Facebook where you can bring back to life important events that happened on this day, years ago. Brands can use this feature to share information about past events in their company's history. Personal profiles can use it to mention a long-lasting friendship or anything else they find important to note and remember from their followers.

Repost

Repost is a feature for the lazy ones. If you are left with no inspiration, you can find and share other posts from fellow creators. Or you can hype your latest post and get more engagement. There is nothing complicated about this feature but it can be a very helpful tool if you have nothing else to post on your channel.

Support Small Business & Order food

To help small businesses around the world in the wake of a pandemic, Instagram introduced two important story stickers - 'Support Small Business' and 'Food Order'.

The new 'Support Small Business' sticker encourages people to show their love for the businesses they enjoy. Instagram users can mention businesses directly to give their followers a quick overview of a business account of their choice. This sticker gives businesses an opportunity to reach a new audience and therefore discover new customers.

The 'Food Order' sticker was introduced by the platform to help small businesses in the food order industry. In order to use this sticker, your business will need to set up food orders with a partner that Instagram approves. When someone taps the sticker in your Instagram story, this person will be redirected to the partner's website where they can order food directly from your restaurant.

Gift Cards

This sticker is only available in some countries so do not be surprised if you don't have access to it. If you are lucky enough to have the 'Gift Card' sticker in your Instagram story, you can use it to set up gift cards on Instagram that your followers can buy to support your business. This is another way for people to support small businesses during times of uncertainties. When someone taps the sticker, they will be redirected to a partner's site where they will have the option to purchase your gift cards.

How to create stories and highlights for your Instagram?

Instagram stories might have had a bad start when they first got introduced to the platform but they are without a doubt a strong force on the app today.

Even though every story disappears in 24 hours, Instagram has made it possible for users to still showcase their best set of stories by introducing Instagram Highlights.

Instagram Highlights have been used by personal profiles and brands not only to showcase their work but to give a fresh look to their feed and provide easier access to what's important.

There are two ways to create an Instagram story Highlight - from an active story or from archived one. So, you can do it manually while your story is still up or you can turn on the Archive option that will automatically save your stories for future use after they disappear.

If you would like to save an active story follow the guide below:

1. Tap on your active Instagram story that you want to save.
2. Select the "Highlight" option from the lower right corner.
3. If you want to save it to an already existing set of highlights, find this group and click on the highlight bubble.
4. If you have no highlights, you will have the option to create one.
5. Enter the name of the highlight you want to create
6. Tap the blue button "Add".

If you would like to save an archived story follow the guide below:

1. Go to Story Settings
2. Turn on Save Story to Archive
3. Edit an existing highlight set to add your story
4. If you have no other highlights, click on the (+ NEW) available under your biography description.
5. Create a new highlight set by selecting the best shots from your archive
6. Add a name and edit the cover of your future highlight
7. Click Done.

Now that we have this out of the way, let's focus on the more important question - how to create compelling Instagram highlights and stories?

Instagram stories and highlights are about your vision and creativity. So, it is important to add a personal touch when creating them. Whether you are a brand or personal profile, Instagram stories and highlights should represent your brand colors, voice, font and style. Not to mention that it has to have consistency. This is the key to creating a cohesive Instagram profile.

Here are some ideas on how to create stunning Instagram stories that you can later use as a highlight:

- Share a guide
- Tell a story
- Use symbols as a design element
- Use fonts to add variety to your text
- Use Pen tools to create an overlay or background
- Use the Instagram feature called Boomerang
- Add GIFs to add more life to your design
- Create a story template for later

How to create a story template?

Use Canva. Canva is a great platform for creating awesome visual content. It is less complicated than Photoshop and this is one of the reasons why people love it. I recommend Canva to my clients because it can do wonders for their Instagram profile.

With Canva, you can create engaging stories, posts and Highlights for your Instagram page in less than 20 minutes. And the best thing about the app is that you can create custom stories and post templates that you can use and edit later on.

Example of story template using Canva:

1. Open Canva and click on Instagram Story or create a custom document with the proper story resolution - 1080 x 1920 pixels.

2. Experiment with Canva elements and select your main objects for your story template

3. Change the position of the elements

4. Add text

INSTAGRAM
TIPS
HAVE A CLEAR GOAL
KNOW WHAT YOU WANT TO ACHIEVE
WITH YOUR IG PAGE
ADD TEXT

5. Complete your story with more Canva elements

6. Save and share your story

Use Photoshop/Illustrator. If you are familiar with Adobe products such as Photoshop and Illustrator, you might find it interesting to use these apps to create a story template for your Instagram page. Photoshop and Illustrator are both great for people who want to have more control over their design. They can start from scratch or use a pre-existing PSD story template and customize it to be cohesive with their Instagram feed.

Example of story template using Photoshop:

1. Open Photoshop and create a new file with the proper story resolution - 1080 x 1920 pixels.

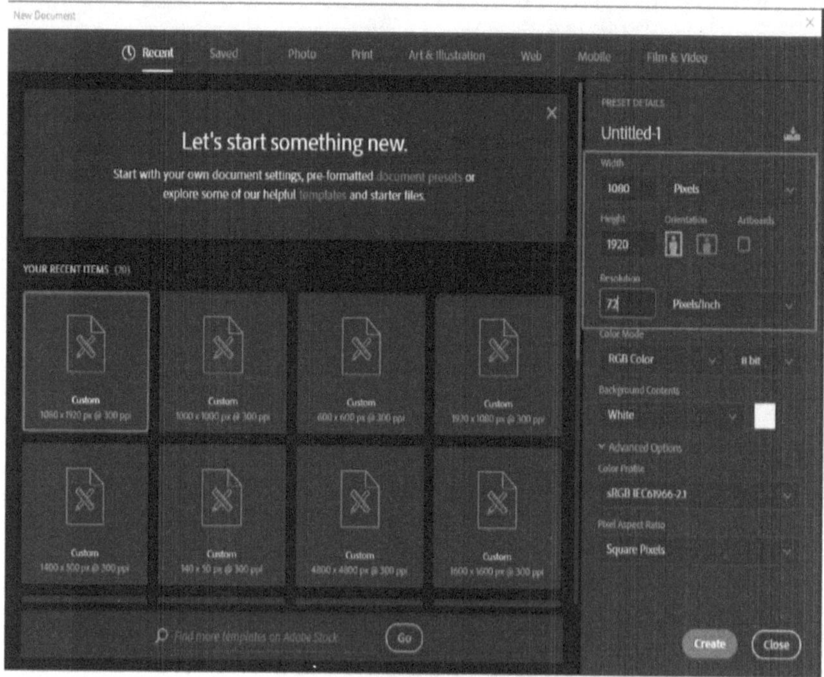

2. Use Photoshop elements to create a frame for your story

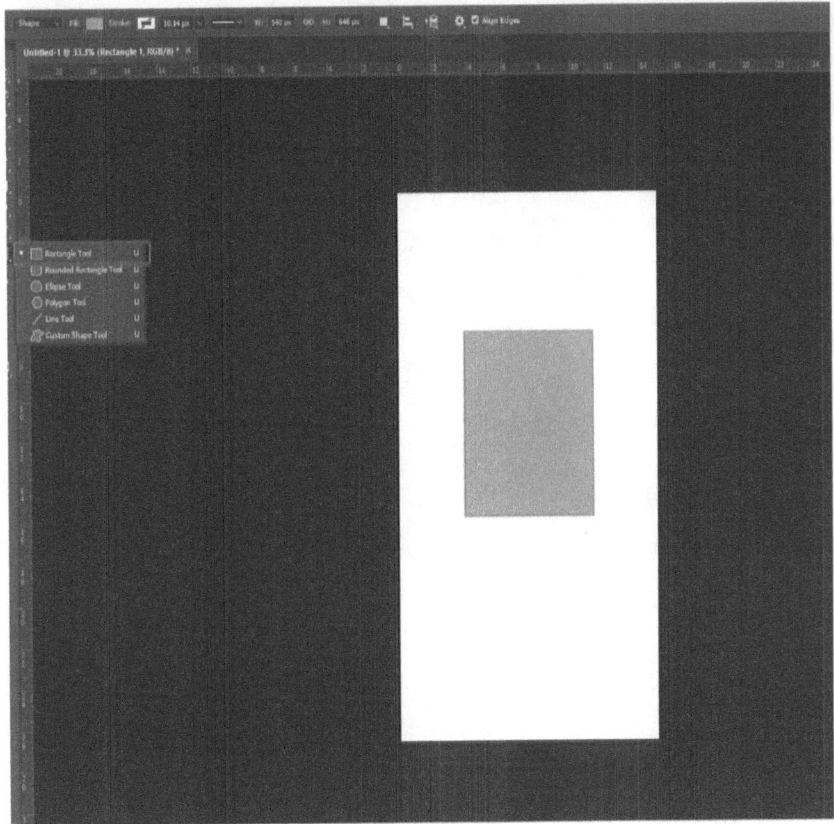

3. Hide the background layer of the file

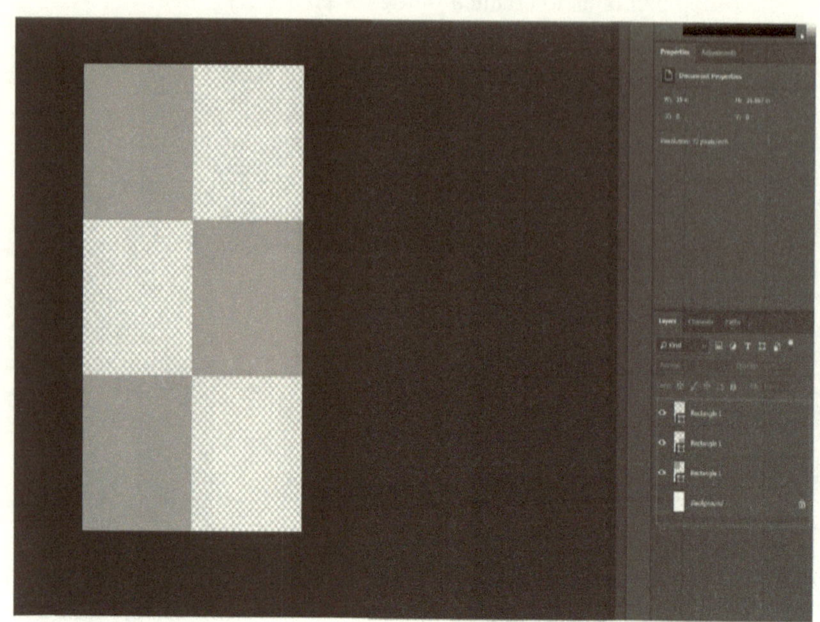

4. Use your own content or add stock photos to the file

5. Style your story – add your brand colors, fonts, etc.

6. Complete your story by adding more elements.

7. Play with the position and color of the elements

WHAT
IS YOUR FAVORITE
DESSERT?

8. You can save the PSD file and use it later on as a story template

Use Adobe Spark. Another Adobe product that is very similar to Canva is Adobe Sparks. You can use the app to create stunning Instagram stories for just a few minutes by editing pre-existing HQ posts.

How to create amazing highlights?

1. Use stock material - photos/icons

Stock photos and icons are great material for Highlights. If you want to stand out and create good Highlights cover for your Instagram, consider using royalty free stock photos or free to use icons.

2. Use Canva or Crello

You can use Canva to create awesome highlights for free. You have the option to choose from pre-existing sets of highlights or start from scratch with the help of free stock photos and elements such as icons, fonts, lines, shapes, etc. The only thing you have to do is create or find a design that aligns with your Instagram feed and you are halfway there.

3. Use Photoshop or Illustrator

If you want to create your own icon and have full control over your highlights, you can also use more advanced editing tools such as Photoshop and Illustrators.

Part 2: Grow your profile - Follow and engage with others

One of my favorite and super-effective ways to increase your Instagram followers and engagement is by leaving genuine and thoughtful comments under other people's posts. This by far one of the best ways to get ORGANIC engagement and growth.

In order to do it the proper way, you need to engage with people in your niche whose content is similar to yours. Find a few small accounts to engage with every day. This will help you build important relationships with other accounts in your niche. But also keep a list of accounts with a bigger fan base that you sometimes comment on. Accounts with hundreds of thousands of followers are also a good choice to consider because the bigger the account, the better exposure you might get. Also, famous accounts attract a lot of likes and plenty of comments. Leaving a nice comment will increase the chance for some of their fans to come your way and become your followers.

Engaging with others includes commenting, liking and following other relevant accounts. Like and follow are simple interactions but this is not the case for comments. If you are a new account, you have no credibility and you still haven't built any relationships with the people in your industry, your comments have to be genuine. You can't just add random emojis and hope that the person will take you seriously. A nice, genuine comment consists of more than four words and it is personalized to the specific profile and post. It is essential that you make the comment personal and if you have no idea how to do that, just read the caption and try to answer/comment on it. You must make it personal, as there are bots that are made to automatically engage with other users by using generic four words or emoticons and a lot of people are aware of that. Avoid looking like a bot!

Remember, if you comment on posts in your niche, there is a very high chance that some of the followers will visit your account and engage with your feed. Do it every day, but not all the time. Don't go crazy with the likes, comments and follows, especially if you are a new account. Instagram can limit your actions. So, try to:

- Like no more than 400 posts per day
- Follow/unfollow no more than 100-160 people per day
- Comment no more than 50 comments per day.

If you fail to follow Instagram limitations and do lots of actions in a short period of time, Instagram will flag your account because of your spam activity. Your account might even get temporarily banned. If such a thing happens, you won't be able to engage with others until your ban is off.

A very effective method to get more initial engagement is to engage with others 15-20 minutes before posting your content and repeat the process for the same amount of time, right after you post. Make sure to take short breaks, so you don't get restricted.

If you have no idea where to find relevant accounts to engage with, try looking at some of the hashtags you use in your posts. Look and engage with accounts who appear at 'Top posts' of your favorite hashtags instead of 'Most recent' posts. Don't be afraid to engage with the followers of your competitors but also, know your boundaries. Don't be annoying and don't behave like a spammy account.

Following and engaging with others should be included in your strategy, but cannot be the only thing that you are doing. A combination with 3-5 good hashtags sets (where each consists of 20-30 hashtags), quality content and engaging with others will get you way further compared to doing only one of them over and over again. It is fascinating how much this can benefit you and how easy it is to see results with a few nice comments and a bunch of likes. Remember to like and comment only if you feel that the post deserves your attention and is relevant to your industry.

Part 2: Grow your profile - Use location (geotag)

Another unique and effective way to reach more people and increase your local awareness is by adding geotags/location tag to your posts. If you want to have more reach and impressions, using the location tag will help you get discovered.

There are two ways to geotag a photo - by tagging the location to your post or by adding it to your Instagram story. The difference between these two is that Instagram stories disappear, so you have limited time to show your account under a certain geotag. On posts, your geotag will last but you will have to be consistent, in order to see progress. Location tag can be extremely helpful for brands, but it can also be used by personal profiles, interested in branding themselves or building a local fanbase.

As a brand

Tagging your location can give your business just the boost it needs. First, it will help you reach more people and there is a very high chance that some of them are going to be in your target group. If you have a physical facility where you offer products or any type of service, it can help you increase the number of customers and sales. If you have an address and people are using your geotag, you can see what kind of people are using your services and visiting your place. This will help you get to know your target group better. You can use this information to optimize your business and improve your online presence.

With geotag, more people will find out about your business. And today, almost every brand has a Social Media account with their details and contact information which will give them extra credibility.

As a personal profile

Branding yourself can be hard, but using the geotag makes it easier. If you tag your location often, your profile will get exposure from other people living / visiting the same area. Some might follow, some might not. With time, you will surely increase your followers and people will start recognizing you on Instagram and maybe in real life. This can open a lot of opportunities for you. For example, if you are a freelance writer, you might get contacted by an agency, interested in your work or someone who needs your services – a new client. It might set you for something else - collaboration with local brands.

There are a lot of new brands entering the market every year. New brands need a lot of exposure. If they are selling locally, there is a very high chance for them to contact a person with followers from the area where their main customers are coming from.

Part 2: Grow your profile - Contests & Giveaways

Organizing a successful contest or a good giveaway can do wonderful stuff to your account, no matter your industry. You can reach thousands of people for free, increase your followers, multiply your engagement, at the cost of giving a reward to some of your followers. Giveaways and raffles are a nice and easy trick for both personal and company profiles to grow their followers faster but not all of the Instagrammers use it. In fact, only 2% of them use this approach regularly.

How to organize a contest/giveaway?

There are many different contests that you can run and all of them will return both followers and engagement. So, the first step for you is to determine the prize for the winner and how suitable it is for your target group. Once you know the answer to this question, you will need to pick the type of giveaway/contest and set the requirements that every participant needs to follow in order to be considered for the final prize. The easier you make the requirements; the more people will join your giveaway.

Giveaway/Contests types

You can be very creative when organizing a giveaway but if you have no idea where to start, here are the most common types:

Engagement based. The requirements for this type of a giveaway are pretty straight forward - in order to be considered as a participant, your audience will have to like or comment on your giveaway post in order to join and have the chance to win. These contests are excellent for increasing the engagement rate of your account and growing your audience.

Tag a friend giveaway. Another great way to increase the number of your followers and reach more of your target audience is by organizing a tag giveaway where users are required to tag friends in order to be considered for the prize. This type of a giveaway usually includes the rules of the engagement based giveaway where you also have to follow the account, like and/or comment on the specific giveaway post. Tag a friend giveaways are a smart way to increase the number of your followers and attract more of your target audience to your Instagram account.

Group giveaway. If you know other people in your niche, you can host a giveaway together. The idea behind group giveaways is to get the maximum exposure for the ones organizing it. As such, every host should repost the giveaway with identical instructions to their own Instagram profile, allowing their own fanbase to engage with the post. Group giveaways can be used by brands and personal profiles to reach a specific demographic and increase awareness. Remember to include a rule to follow EACH host.

Creative (User-generated) Contest. If you own an Instagram account, based on displaying your art, then running a creative contest can be a good fit for you. It can be photography, art, makeup, selfies, challenge contests, where your followers are required to do a specific thing and use your branded hashtag to enter with their own content. Creative contests are great for getting a branded hashtag more popular and get your account some more visibility and awareness.

Product giveaway/contest. A very beneficial collaboration between brands and personal profiles is organizing a giveaway/contest together. In such a giveaway/contest, the brand is responsible to provide the products for the giveaway while the personal profile has the responsibility to attract as many people as possible. Most of the product giveaways and contests are engagement based which makes them great for brands and personal profiles looking for more exposure and growth.

Website giveaway. You can use Instagram to promote your giveaway and bring extra traffic to your website. For example, you can announce your giveaway on Instagram with a post using the caption: "To enter - click the link in our bio". This will encourage people to visit your website and sign for what you are offering. However, because website giveaways are mostly used for sales funnels with an effort to exclude the prospects uninterested in what you have to offer, the number of participants can be lower than the rest options. This can be very beneficial for brands, looking for quality leads.

Loop giveaway. If group giveaway is the perfect option for personal profiles, loop giveaway is the alternative for brands. This type of giveaway includes multiple brands (it can be 5, it can be 20) working and hosting a giveaway together. Similar to group giveaways, all hosts are required to share the giveaway post with the exact instructions to their Instagram page. To get a better idea, here is how a loop giveaway would work if 3 brands were hosting it - Account 1 will post the giveaway post and direct people to Account 2 to follow; Account 2 will post the giveaway post and direct people to Account 3 to follow; Account 3 will post the giveaway post and direct people to Account 1 to follow, hence, a complete loop. The goal of a loop giveaway is to get more long-term followers, interested in your brand and increase your overall brand awareness. Loop giveaways can be very successful but very time-consuming to organize. In order to go smoothly, you would want to select someone who would be in charge of organizing the giveaway and making sure everyone is on the same page.

Although every giveaway will give you results, it is important to choose the best fit for your needs.

The best performing type for small brands (5k - 30k followers) are tag-a-friend and product giveaways as well as creative contests. Bigger brands can take advantage of website and product giveaways while personal profiles can use creative contests, product and group giveaways.

Once you have the idea, the next thing you need to take care of is to set how long the contest/giveaway will last for. Do not run it for more than two/three weeks as people will forget about it. You want your giveaway/contest to have the desirable element that will make people follow the rules in order to join it. It is important to make it believable for your audience - a limited opportunity everyone can win.

If you want to show to your followers your account is trustworthy, it is best to make it very clear when you are going to announce the lucky winners. Keep in mind that your followers are not in the same time zone, so make sure that you add an extra clarification on the time.

The very last two steps are to make a set of hashtags that you will be using plus the design of the contest.

Hashtags

A combination of three types of hashtags must be used in your giveaway post to get to your target group:

   • Your industry hashtags - you are a business about hats, then feel free to use at least 5 hashtags that will bring the right target to your post - the hat lovers.

   • Giveaway hashtags - community hashtags such as #giveaway and #contest can be very helpful, as there is a big number of people who would like to win what you have to offer. But be careful when you use them as they can attract people from all niches. If possible, search for a hashtag that specifies the type of your giveaway. For example, if you are offering a makeup product giveaway, try to use #makeupgiveaway instead of #giveaway.

• Branded hashtag - whether you have them as a requirement or not, using a branded hashtag as part of your giveaway post is definitely a must.

Design

The design of your post is the very first thing your followers will notice when your giveaway/contest is posted. So, you would want to make your design catchy, using bright colors and easy to read with a text announcing the giveaway. This is how you can make sure that while people are scrolling through their feed, they will for sure stop and look at your post. Here are two examples of a giveaway post:

Giveaway example (personal profile):

Contest example (brand):

During the giveaway, it is essential to remind your followers to participate. That does not mean that you have to post about it every day, but you can add it to your story, highlights, create a countdown post such as "Only three days left to Join and Win…." .

End

Once the giveaway is over, you can draw the winner, using a third-party software. You can announce the lucky winners in a new post, add it to your story or start a LIVE video. Doing it in front of other people will prove that you have good intentions and will lower the chance of accounts unfollowing you, once the contest is over.

Note: If you no longer need the giveaway post, you can archive it. If you want to keep it to your Instagram feed, you can edit the caption by removing the rules and adding the winners to avoid confusion when people find your giveaway post in the future.

Aftermath

If you have to pay from your own money to make the giveaway or give your products to get more visibility and followers, let me tell you this: At the end of the day, you are the real winner! Thousands of brands are paying a crazy amount of money to their Social Media experts to attract the right people (target group) to their brand. While you are the one using only one of your products to:

1. Attract more of your target group

2. Increase your followers

3. Get "FREE" (the cost of one product) exposure

4. A chance to get featured on the Explore page which is equal to even more discovery.

5. Plus, you might even get an increase in sales.

Instagram is a platform that won't hold you down and limit your giveaway creativity. As long as you are on good terms with their policy, you can be as creative as you want and the result will be the one to determine how good the giveaway/contest turned out to be. Remember to pay attention to your account's analytics.

Quick Tip: If your giveaway/contest is not performing well, try investing in Instagram ads.

Part 2: Grow your profile - Cross-promote on other Social Media platforms

If you happened to have another Social Media account with an engaging audience, chances are these people are not following you everywhere. You can try to combine both audiences with an effort to increase your Instagram followers by encouraging your audience to find and follow you there. Cross-promotion is a great way to attract people who you know are interested in your product.

How to combine the audience of two different platforms?

There are many ways to connect two Social Media accounts, some are paid, some are free. Here are a few suggestions to understand this method better:

If you are a YouTuber, mention it in your videos. Try to make it look natural. Encouraging people to come from one platform to another is not an easy task, so don't get discouraged if the process is not as fast as you wish.

If you are a blogger, add a sidebar with your Instagram feed. There are plugins (on Wordpress) that can help you display your recent 3-6-9 posts. People do look at the sidebars and if they like what they see, you might end up with a new follower.

If you are a company, offering physical stuff, add your Instagram account to the label of your product. You can add a QR code that leads to your Instagram account.

If you are using only a Facebook page, but you want to have an Instagram account to explore a broader audience, running a giveaway with a requirement to follow your brand on Instagram could work great too. The terms of the giveaway must mention clicking the follow button on your Instagram account.

You have an advantage if you are using the same username everywhere. The rest depends on your creativity and how you will encourage your followers to like your other channels. If this is not something you are very good at, you can hire a Social Media expert that will create a strategy for your accounts. If you are not interested and you have a personal account, you can always choose the next thing on the list - inviting people.

To invite people you will need to have your Facebook account connected to your Instagram. That way you can see how many of your friends you aren't following on Instagram and you can also invite people who aren't on Instagram. And if that isn't enough, you can also connect your Instagram profile with your phone contacts and discover even more familiar accounts that would like to follow you.

If done right, cross-promotion is a great way to expand your Instagram audience by attracting people already familiar with your brand and products.

Part 2: Grow your profile - Paid advertising

You can grow your account by the old fashioned way - paid advertising. Instagram advertising is the only right way to boost your account if you are interested in growing your channel fast. You can use it to achieve different objectives such as get a lot of exposure, drive traffic to your website, help you reach new people, boost your engagement (legally) and more. But don't get too excited, it will definitely take you some time to find the best combination of the right target group and the perfect attention-grabbing ad style.

Instagram advertising options can be accessed only by Professional accounts - Businesses and Creators because they are the ones tight with Facebook Page and ad account, where you set the payment and get to the advanced settings of Instagram advertising.

Before you are certain Instagram advertisement is the way to go, you need to understand that paid advertising is situational. It is suitable for most of the industries - from fitness and yoga gurus to eCommerce shops. However, Instagram's new policies do not allow content that promotes unrealistic claims about diet/weight loss products. Some of these new rules also restrict the promotion of weight loss products and cosmetic procedures to users under 18.

Paid advertising can also be good for personal profiles who already found a way to monetize their profile (earn money). Advertising is in order if you have a goal you want to accomplish. Otherwise, you are just wasting your money instead of focusing on growing your profile. Having made that clear, let's see when you should be interested in promoting your account on Instagram?

If you would like to tell your customers that you can be found

on Instagram. There are many people who follow you on Facebook, Twitter or Instagram, but most of them follow you on only one of the social media platforms. Paid advertising is great for cross-promotion. It is also an amazing chance for you to show your audience that you can be found on multiple platforms. With time, people will recognize you more and this (brand recognition) is generally something you want.

If you are about to launch a new product. Instagram is now partnering with Shopify, which gives you an opportunity to tag your products and have a shop tap directly on this platform. Advertising your products on Instagram can be a very powerful tool to multiply shop sales, as long as you know your target group.

For personal profiles, it might be an affiliate program they want to promote.

If you want to reach more people and increase your brand awareness. Once again, this is perfect for startups and brands in general. You can drive attention to your app, product or services with the help of these types of ads.

If you want more engagement or traffic to your website. Similar to the Business side of Facebook, on Instagram, you can select the objective called "Engagement". It is effective to either promote your Instagram account or a specific post. You can also promote your video and drastically increase your video views.

If you want to collect leads or conversions. Instagram ads will also allow your business to collect leads with personal information such as email addresses, full names, etc. You can use paid ads to increase your sales too.

You can choose different ads, depending on the objective you want to achieve. There are 4 types of ads that you can create on Instagram - photo, video, carousel and story ads. Instagram stories ads can be either a single image or a single video. My personal favorites are photo and video ads as they turn the most profit and they are a safe choice. A carousel ad might not perform that good and a story ad is easy to exit.

How to run a successful campaign?

A lot of people advertise on the platform, but only a few do it right. In order to have a successful campaign, the key is to test, test and test. You can either test multiple designs on one demographic group or change the demographic groups and test the same image. It is in your hands to choose your audience based on location, age, gender, demographics, interests or behavior. You can even choose to target people who have a relationship with your customers or interact with your account. Look at the result of each of your ads and determine which set is worth having your attention.

When you know your target group, spend some time on creating the best and most appropriate ad design for the selected target group. The more creative you are, the better ROI (Return on investment) you will get. Never forget that Instagram is a visual platform, so create stunning designs with the help of high-quality (or stock) photos. Try to create an ad that doesn't look like an ad. People love natural, easy-going content rather than a blatant product promotion that will turn into a bad campaign.

If you have no idea what to do, take advantage of the features that Instagram offers like Boomerang (mini videos) and Layout (combine multiple photos into one). Or go through your Instagram feed and take a look at what your audience likes the most. Create an ad based on that post and watch your account grow!

Make sure to create an ad design that stands out. Use bright colors and moving stories to grab the attention of your target group. Compelling ad design is key when running a successful ad campaign. Try to hook your potential customers and followers into your ads. If you are promoting your website, create an ad in the same style as your landing page. Double-check if your landing page is loading fast and make sure it is good-looking with a modern touch, so you can get better results.

Choosing the right marketing objective, ad style (carousel, story, etc.) and design is just as important as writing a good ad caption. A good caption can be long or short but it has to be meaningful. You can choose to be entertaining or tell a serious story as long as it is capturing your audience's attention. Finish the caption with a strong CTA (call to action) message to get the best results.

Brands - Sponsored posts

If you don't have the budget for a big ad campaign, there is something else you can do - offer a Sponsored post. To do such a post, you will need to find and reach out to an influencer in your niche, willing to promote your product to their audience. Most of the influencers are satisfied with getting a free sample of your product, but bigger accounts might require payment.

To find an influencer, you can hire someone to curate a list with suitable people or you can use websites like Ninja Outreach, which will give you the chance to sort and filter influencers by different categories (tags).

Note: Beware! There are a lot of fake influencers, so before working with one, spend a few minutes observing whether he has fake followers or if he is part of a POD.

It is understandable if Instagram is not your first choice to run a paid campaign, but the creativity that the platform gives you will surprise you. The budget you set will be the one that will be used - not less, NEVER more. Once your campaign is ready for the world, make sure to keep an eye on how it is performing. Analytics is the best way to optimize your current and future ad campaigns.

Part 2: Grow your profile - Collaborations

(personal profiles)

There is no fun in growing alone - networking and building relationships is part of the job. And while replying to comments can help you build a community, you will also need to connect with fellow creators in your industry. Why?

Working with others can give you a lot of opportunities, fun moments and help you reach more people, which is equal to more followers. And as someone who wants to grow their Instagram, you would want to attract as many followers as possible, especially when you know that they are the right target for your account.

When two (or more) Social Media accounts work together, it is called collaboration. There are two types of collaborations on Instagram. The first type is between two or more influencers (personal profiles), where the idea of both sides is to grow their accounts. The other type is the collaboration between brands and influencers, which will be discussed later in this book.

The best way to start looking for people to collaborate with is to know what to look for. For example, you want to work with someone who is close to your range of followers. Although it is nice to work with the big accounts from your niche, the chances of them wanting to work with you are not very optimistic. But it is not only about the followers – you also need to be sure that the audience of your future collaboration will be interested in your account. Otherwise, the collaboration won't be as successful. There is no point in working with someone who won't benefit from showing your content to their uninterested audience and the same goes for the other way around. So, always check these three variables before reaching out to a fellow influencer:

1. Check their account – are the posts similar to yours or do you have anything in common (i.e. you can be both comedians and that's pretty much enough).

2. Check their audience - the comments from their followers (a quick scan) and some of their profiles.

3. Check their biography – if their account has a clear and aesthetic look and the link in their biography is "safe to click".

Once you have found the perfect match, do not stop. Instead, try to collect a list of names that you want to collaborate with. When the list is done, you can start reaching out to your top choices. The best approach is to find their emails and even though DMs (direct messages on Instagram) can do the work, it is a business collab (short for collaboration) and nothing says good manners like sending a nice, well-structured email. You will most likely find their email through their profile, other social platforms or their website. If you can't find it anywhere, it would be okay to send them a DM (Direct Message) instead.

The message should contain: a compliment to their hard work (the more detailed, the better), why it is a good idea to collaborate and the details of your account. If you already have something in mind, it would be a great idea to share it too. Creators think outside of the box, so don't worry if your idea sounds crazy. Try to make a catchy offer the other person won't resist, which should be relatively easy, considering the fact that you are in the same industry.

Here are some suggestions for successful collaborations:

1. Do a Takeover – swap each other's accounts for a limited time. Takeovers are great and effective because you are offering a piece of what you do to a new audience. They can be done through posts or Instagram stories. Making an interesting introduction and offering an exciting, entertaining day can boost your account a lot. But, it can turn against you and lose some of your followers if you do it for more than a few days.

2. Make a video together. This type of collaboration has been known for years and here is why - video speaks louder than any nice, perfectly taken picture. And as long as the video is entertaining and has a good quality, you can get plenty of viewers and nice engagement. To be most effective, you have to post it to both of your profiles. And you can even add it to IGTV.

3. Post pictures with one another. A great way to draw interest to both Instagram profiles is by posting and tagging pictures with the person you are collaborating with. If you offer both of your audiences nice and catchy captions, you have higher chances to get attention to each other's profiles.

4. Run a group giveaway or a contest. Another very successful way to grow your profiles is by organizing a giveaway/contest together. To get the most out of a giveaway, it is best if you work with more than one person. A group of collaborators will give your account a bigger exposure than you can imagine. And that is not all - making it a requirement to follow all the hosts of the giveaway/contest will get you more followers, in no time. Just make sure that the prize is worth it - the better the prize you are offering, the more people will want to participate.

5. Start a challenge together. You never know what is the next trending thing - it might be a challenge that you've started. Even if it doesn't go viral, you will have a clear idea of how engaging your audience is and have a lot of fun while doing it.

6. Run an Instagram page together. If you enjoy working with someone and you are a total match you don't need to stop after one collaboration. What you can do is create a page and manage it together. It can be about something that you both love or a new, different topic.

7. Do a Q&A while broadcasting LIVE on Instagram . It is more fun when you do Q&A with someone, especially if it is live. If your followers feel the good vibes between the two of you and the Q&A has been promoted before, many will join the live stream.

If this is your first collaboration and you don't have any idea to pitch (offer) to the other influencer, do not worry – you will figure it out together. That's why collaborations are always a win – you can build a new relationship and grow your account, while having fun and socializing with people with the same interests as yours. Don't be afraid to take the first step. You might be surprised how many people will be interested in your offer.

Part 2: Grow your profile - Shoutouts

Instagram is a platform that gives you a lot of opportunities to grow and brand yourself. With over a billion active users on the platform, variety is guaranteed. You can find accounts in many industries, each of them targeting a different niche market. And, with so many active users, there is no wonder that there are accounts that curate the best content in each niche and share it with their followers. This is done in the form of a shoutout/feature.

A shoutout is posting the content of other people on your own Instagram by crediting them. This way the followers of the shoutout account will have the chance to see your picture and react to it. Shoutouts are great to bring more followers and increase your engagement. How to get a shoutout?

There are two main things that you can do to increase your chances of getting a shoutout - find your niche and add the hashtag of the shoutout account to your current hashtag set. This hashtag is branded and most of the time, shoutout accounts will have it in their account's bio description. If you are a fan of the page and you constantly engage with their content, there is a very big chance for you to get featured.

It is very important to find your niche. For example, if you have a dog Instagram (yes, it is a thing), there is a very big chance to find a channel, that features dogs, if you are a travel blogger, you might find a travel account who would like to feature your content, if you are a makeup artist, there are also many channels that will shout out your creative pictures too.

One of the biggest, most famous platforms that can help you grow faster is 9gag. Although their main account is still very active on Instagram, they also have different accounts for the different niches - for couples, for travelers, for dog lovers, for cat lovers, etc. If your content has the viral element they look for, you can get a feature and get thousands of likes and new followers.

However, getting featured on a channel with millions of fans and people wanting to get featured is very rare. Chances are that you will never get there. {Although, if this is your goal, you will find a way to achieve it!}

To compromise, there is something else you can do - go for channels that just like yours, are still growing. There are many channels between 10 000 - 500 000 followers that will be more than happy to have your content on their feed.

How to find accounts willing to feature me?

You can start by looking at your competitors. There is a very high possibility that they are tagging accounts through their captions or by tagging their pictures. You can also check the posts they have been tagged on. Once you find a suitable account for your content, it is important to like and leave some nice comments here and there and of course, hit their follow button. If shoutouts are your goal, you can even take a step further and look at the biography section of their account. Some of them will have their own hashtags, which you will have to include in your post. Every page has its own hashtags to make it easier to find content when curating their future posts. To find what type of hashtag to use, you can look at the page biography or in their caption, when a shoutout is uploaded. Most of the accounts will have some information on how to get featured. If not, you can always contact them and ask them for their requirements.

Do not be surprised if some of the accounts ask you for money, in order to get featured. This method works well with accounts that have built their engagement from the bottom, without using fake followers. Unfortunately, it is hard to tell which account is using bots without additional help - online software that will show how many fake followers are there compared to the real one. Chances are that the best websites that offer this type of services are paid. A free alternative is finding an Instagram engagement calculator online that will calculate the engagement rate of their accounts and give you the data in percentages.

If you, like me, think that this is too much work, you are not wrong! That's why my suggestion is to focus on the accounts that won't cost you any money. After all, there is no guarantee that if you pay you are going to attract thousands of followers. Some shoutouts work, while others don't. My accounts have been featured so many times and only some of these times I got good results. But once you get a good shoutout, you will see that it is totally worth it.

The success rate of a shoutout is hard to determine. However, if there is an increase in your profile visits, followers and engagement on your recent posts, the shoutout is working.

One extra bit of advice:

When you get a shoutout from an account that did it as a free will, show them some love, if not by following them, by tagging them to your Instagram story. This way the account will be thankful to you and you might get featured again soon. Not only that, but it will give you some credibility in front of the followers that see your stories on a daily basis. After all, you just got a shoutout!

Part 2: Grow your profile - Edit your pictures

When you consistently create content for your Instagram, it is best to have a filter/style for your posts so they have the same color scheme and exposure (brightness, contrast, shadow, etc.). Have you ever seen a post in your Instagram newsfeed, so recognizable that without looking at the name of the creator you already know exactly who's post this is?

This is most likely because the person is using a consistent filter to their content. It is a very smart trick to use in order to make your content easily recognizable and memorable. This effect can be done with the help of editing tools such as Lightrooom (specifically presets) or Instagram UI.

You can edit your pictures directly on Instagram. The platform offers filters and a lot of editing options such as brightness, contrasts, shadows, and highlights. For best results, you would want to use every one of the four options and add a nice filter once you are done adjusting the exposure of your image. Filters such as Valencia and Aden will help you stick to a color scheme that fits your Instagram. If the filter is too intense for your content, you can adjust it by tapping once on it and decrease its opacity.

Instagram UI is a great way to learn more about editing your content, but if you want to take your account professionally, adjusting the light and adding a filter might not be enough. Instead, you might need to use editing software that gives you more to play with.

There are some amazing mobile apps and desktop tools that can help you edit your pictures. For example, PicsArt is a great mobile app that can give you a lot of additional options to choose from. You can use different filters and hide imperfections very easily with the help of this app.

If you are looking for more than just a basic edit and you have some extra time to invest in something new, then Photoshop and Lightroom are the way to go. With Photoshop, you will have limitless options to edit and improve your content, hide imperfections and even delete people from your pictures. While Lightroom will help you finalize your content by choosing the right exposure and presets for your content. Presets are similar to Instagram filters with the minor difference that you can create your own or download them from others. They are like the perfect filter for your content that you apply with just one click.

But it will take time before you start feeling comfortable using these two

Adobe products. Fortunately enough, there are many tutorials on the Internet that are free and are willing to help you get into the basics of these awesome platforms.

The biggest problem of raw pictures is that very often they do not match your Instagram theme and style. And they can look a lot better with just a little bit of editing. Sometimes, lack of natural light can stop us from getting the best content for our Instagram feed. When such a thing happens, you can use editing software like Lightroom to improve your raw pictures before uploading them to Instagram. This can drastically improve your content and make your feed look much better. People love seeing a consistent style and edited pictures look much better.

But don't edit too much, after all, you don't make your picture look fake. More professional looking pictures will attract a lot of new people to your profile and will make them stay longer in your account, looking at your work (feed). Having a consistent style for your Instagram feed will make you much more recognizable among your followers. Plus, high-quality pictures often get better engagement and grow faster.

Part 2: Grow your profile - Ask for feedback

Once you get more followers, who like your pictures on a daily basis, you will notice that some of your posts are performing much better compared to others. It is important to pay attention to those patterns so you know what your audience prefers. Sometimes, it might be hard to determine the reason why your posts get more engagement. If you are not sure what to post next on your feed, you might ask your followers for feedback.

Receiving feedback from your followers can help you curate and schedule content for the rest of the month. It will help you understand the type of content they find most engaging and you will know what to focus on. Is it the funny pictures that you post, is it the informative video that you upload from time to time or maybe it's when you compare 4 different pictures and ask your followers to choose which one is the best. It differs from account to account. It works extremely well for brands that post various types of content - ambassadors (and influencers), product photos, videos, funny pictures, etc. But it could also do great work for a personal profile, because the end goal is to make your next posts perform better than anything before.

When you are asking for feedback, you will need to find the right approach to your audience. There are two ways to do that without being too pushy and losing your followers. The first one is by creating a post with the different type of content that you use and ask your followers to choose which one they enjoy the most. To get more responses, you will have to make it easy to participate. For example, add "Pick a number" or "Choose A,B,C,D", so it is encouraging and at the same time not that time-consuming.

Ask for feedback Example (brand):

The second type that you can use is the Instagram story. You can create a poll and ask people to choose between two different types of content or use the quiz sticker and add up to 4 options. This is great if your profile has less variety. However, stories disappear after 24H, so it is limited to time, which might not be enough time for your followers to participate and you might miss an important vote. That's why using polls on stories can be repeated over a certain amount of time (once per two weeks is great), but not too often. Stories can give you better results as they are easier to engage with compared to leaving a comment on a post.

Once you know what to focus on, it is important to don't ignore it. Don't go on autopilot posting the content you've decided to post. Listen to the feedback and take a step back to see how your people react to your posts. If the numbers of your "survey" are close and there are two types of content that your followers love, then focus on delivering both of them and limit the rest.

And although, listening to feedback will help you grow and make your followers more loyal, do not forget to tease people with fresh and exciting new content while you also have the not so exciting posts once in a while. Otherwise, too much excitement and the same hype over and over again might get annoying to your followers and instead of growing, you will see a decrease in your followers.

Remember: Instagram requires a lot of patience and balance, just like life.

Part 2: Grow your profile - IGTV

IGTV is a great Instagram feature that allows users to share video content designed for mobile-optimized viewing of longer videos. Unlike the regular Instagram posts, IGTV videos support both vertical and landscape size content. The length of one IGTV video also differs from the post you share on your feed. Regular posts, shared on your feed, can be up to 1 minute while IGTV content is between 1 and 10 minutes long.

Instagram users can upload up to 10 minutes long videos on IGTV from their phones. If you have a verified Instagram account, you can upload up to 60 minutes long videos from your computer.

There are two options to get on IGTV - through your personal/business Instagram account or through the IGTV app. Both of them use your Instagram profile. You can find the IGTV app on your phone's app store or if you prefer to stay on the Instagram app, you can also find IGTV from the Explore page of the app.

What is so special about IGTV?

Brands and personal profiles use IGTV to share longer video clips and create better content that would result in bigger exposure and discovery for their Instagram account. Video content is extremely popular on Instagram because it offers users to showcase their personalities, creativity, and stories in a compelling manner. Plus, videos are much more captivating and interesting than image posts and that is one of the reasons people love them.

IGTV is a great tool to expand your Instagram audience. Instagram users can engage with your video by liking and leaving a comment and they can also share it, just like a regular post.

How is IGTV different from Instagram LIVE?

IGTV and Instagram LIVE are great for engaging with your audience and even though they might look similar to each other, they have some key differences.

With IGTV, you can prepare content in advance and share it at a specific time. While Instagram LIVE is being streamed in real-time. You can answer comments in real-time, which makes Instagram LIVE a tool to connect with your audience. However, because Instagram LIVE is part of Instagram stories, your Instagram LIVE video will last only for 24hours whereas IGTV video will stay on your channel for as long as you want.

IGTV Insights & Important Metrics

IGTV is still relatively new on the app, so there is plenty of space for creativity and experiments with the content you create.

While IGTV's Insights are not as detailed as post and profile insights, you can still use them to learn a lot from your video's performance and understand what works and what doesn't for your channel. The most important IGTV metrics that you must know about are:

- Viewer Count (Views) - the number of views indicates the total number of people who have interacted with your IGTV video. A view is counted when someone spends more than 3 seconds watching your video.
- Engagement - a combination of the number of likes and comments your IGTV has
- Audience Retention Graph (Average Percentage Watched) - a detailed visual representation of the percentage of all views a video has including the peaks and lows of your IGTV video.

You can use these insights to get a hint of what your audience wants to see the most from you.

To get access to IGTV Insights:

1. Tap on the video you want to analyze
2. Select the option menu, available at the bottom of the video
3. Tap 'View Insights'

How to get started with IGTV?

Choose the main topic of your IGTV channel. Before you start your IGTV channel, you need to determine the type of content you want to share. Think of the topic that matters the most to you if you want to find the most appropriate subject. Choose something that you feel comfortable talking about and you would not get sick of. Keep in mind the target group you want to attract to your IGTV.

Select the tone of IGTV. The tone of your channel is also important to consider before you create your first IGTV. Choose the right voice for your channel and make sure it aligns with the content you are planning to share. Pick the right tone - would it be catchy, quirky, inspirational, informative, formal, etc. Determine the length of your IGTV videos and think of a couple of content ideas for your channel.

Prepare a few videos in advance. Do a research on the topic you have chosen so you start working on video material. Study your niche and find what is trending in your industry. Allow your viewers to help you with content ideas as well. Creating video content on a daily basis can be very exhausting. Video footage is more demanding than regular Instagram posts. So before you take a spoon that is too big for your mouth, make sure to find out how long it takes you to produce one video and will you be able to keep the same speed for a year, maybe more?

Edit your videos. There is no secret that longer videos require editing. If there is one sure way to make your videos more exciting, it is with the help of catchy sound effects, stickers, filters and other video settings. You can also remove noisy background sounds, cut wrong lines, remove unnecessary material and everything else you can think of to make your IGTV video on point. Create a routine of the way you edit videos. This will ensure that your videos are following the same style.

Creating quality video content isn't hard with IGTV. You can use your phone to shoot your video, edit it and upload it directly. Or use your computer to do it. IGTV works on desktop as well, so you can share content from your PC as well.

Quick Tip: You can use Facebook Creator Studio to post content on your IGTV channel.

When your content is ready, remember to prepare your post the best way possible.

Add hashtags. Once the video is ready to be published, make sure to add hashtags. Just like stories and posts, IGTV also uses hashtags. So make sure to include only a few, strategic but relevant hashtags to your video.

Optimize your content. Don't forget to use the clickable link in the descriptions of your IGTV videos. This is a great way to drive traffic to a website of your choice (your blog, landing page, etc.). Adding your own link to IGTV is accessible by all Instagram accounts, no matter the size. Remember to select a catchy cover for your IGTV.

Promote your content. To bring more attention to your fresh post, consider sharing your IGTV to your Instagram feed. Find the best part of your IGTV video and publish it as a regular Instagram post. The main idea of this practice is to grab the attention of your Instagram followers after the very first seconds of playing. If the snippet you have chosen is captivating enough, your IGTV will be viewed by more people and reach many. You can also share it on your Instagram story for even more visibility.

What to post on IGTV?

The content you create must be associated with your niche, social media and business goals.

Behind the scenes footage. Show your work atmosphere, give an office tour or get creative with your team and prepare fun material for your audience. If you are a personal profile, show something personal and special or give a quick look of what your normal day is about.

Teasers. If you are working on a new project, do not be afraid to share some of the details. Whether it is a blog post, YouTube video, upcoming merchandise release or new project launch, IGTV is a great way to build hype around your new project. Creating a buzz will help you reach more people and convert some of them into sales.

Educational content. One of the best types of content you can share on Social Media is educational. Tutorials and 'How To' guides can provide a lot of value for the regular user. Educational content will help others to solve a particular problem and allow a real and authentic connection with your audience.

Exclusive content. One popular trend amongst IGTV users is the creation of 'series'. Episodic content can perform excellent on the platform and the best thing about it is that everything can be found in one place - on your IGTV feed. If you stay consistent long enough, people will start expecting your next 'show'.

Q&As. Q&A sessions are another great option to show off your personality on IGTV. They are so unique that there are no two Q&A sessions alike. These types of events can immediately impress and build a relationship with your potential target group. For this main reason, Q&A events are great for keeping your audience engaged.

Ask your followers what type of content they want to see. If you already have a group of people dedicated to your Instagram account, use Instagram stories to find out what type of content they want to see on your IGTV channel.

Other IGTV Tips

Shoot vertical videos. Before you share and promote your IGTV content, make sure that your videos look presentable vertically. Even though IGTV allows horizontal videos, the feature is mainly built for vertical ones.

Promote your content outside of Instagram. If your IGTV does not perform well, consider cross promoting your content outside of the app. Once you decide to expand your reach beyond Instagram, you will have a lot of possibilities to discover new people. For example, if you decide to share your IGTV video on Facebook, it will help you gain access to a larger audience that otherwise you would have never reached. The same is true for the rest Social platforms and forums.

Follow your audience. While IGTV covers a lot of different niches, your audience might not be using this feature as regularly as you expect. For example, your target group might not use IGTV as much as they use Instagram stories. So, it is really important to know where your audience is.

Include video subtitles. Make sure to optimize your videos for silent viewing with the help of video subtitles that match the script of your IGTV video. This will not only be beneficial for the viewers who have their sounds off but it will be much more helpful for people with certain disabilities

Stick to what works best. If you discover a specific type of content that performs well on your IGTV channel, stick to this model and use the same pattern to reach as many people as possible. This does not mean to stop being creative. Not at all. Coming up with new, fresh material is always good but it is even better when you mix it with something that you know it will work.

Improve your content every chance you get. Nobody expects from you to be a professional video producer or editor. It takes time to get comfortable with the process of creating videos but it is important to never stop improving. Whether it is to purchase a new photography equipment or discover a new video editing software, working on improving the quality of your videos will bring more people to your channel.

Aim for consistency. Instagram will not work for you if you are not consistent. The same goes for IGTV. Let your audience know how often you will be posting and at what time. Stick to a schedule, so they know when to expect new content.

Engage with others. Discover influential IGTV creators and engage with their content. Share your personal opinion on a certain topic or simply compliment the good work of the creator without sounding too robotic. Use every opportunity you have to interact with your followers and make sure to reply to their comments under your own IGTV videos.

Remember that each niche of the IGTV community is different and what works for some might not work for you. So find your rhythm through research and experiments.

Part 2: Grow your profile - Instagram Reels

In 2020, Instagram introduced a new way to create content and reach new people - Instagram Reels. It enables people to express themselves in a more creative way and discover more of what they love. The feature allows IG users to create and discover 15-seconds videos and share them with their followers or in a new dedicated Feed on the Explore page of Instagram.

The concept of Instagram Reels is similar to another very famous social network - TikTok. The feature encourages users to record and edit fun content with the help of audio, special effects and other creative tools (backgrounds, games, stickers, filters). Reels can be recorded in a series of clips (multiple times) or all at once. If you have video content on your phone, you can upload the footage to the platform as well.

Instagram Reels takes into consideration your profile settings. If you are a private account, you can share a reel to a Feed only your followers can see.

People who see your Reels would not be able to share them with others who don't follow you. On the contrary, if you have a public account, you can share your reel to the special Explore page where it has the potential to be discovered by a huge and diverse audience. And the best thing about it is when your reel gets featured in the Explore page, you will be notified.

Whether you have a private or public account, you can share your reel to your Instagram story and Close Friends as well as send it through direct messages.

Instagram Reels vs. Instagram Stories?

Instagram Reels might sound similar to Instagram Stories but there are a few key differences between the two features.

Audience. Instagram Reels and Stories do not share the same exact audience even though they share the same platform. Instagram stories have been around for much longer and they are widely popular on the app. They are used by many businesses and Influencers in different industries on a regular basis.

Reels is a new feature catered toward the Gen Z of Instagram. While everyone has the chance to create a reel, this might not be the preferred type of content that many decide to share.

Content. Users can share 15-seconds clips on both, Instagram Reels and Stories. However, Instagram Stories is the better option when it comes to sharing images. The focus of Instagram Reels is not on image posts but rather short video content. That's why Reels offer AR effects, speed control, audio settings and the option to align multiple clips for cleaner transitions.

Purpose. Both of the Instagram features, Stories and Reels can be used by users to reach a new audience. With the help of story stickers, you can build a consistent audience over a period of time. But Instagram Stories are an excellent tool to make your existing community even more engaging.

Reels, on the other hand, similar to IGTV and your regular Instagram posts, can bring a lot of attention to your profile in a short period of time. Especially if your content gets on the Explore page.

Effort. There are so many easy ways to create Instagram Stories. You can use the in-app feature Create, an editing tool such as Canva/Sparks or take a picture, upload and customize it to make it more unique. This is not the case for Instagram Reels. Creating video content that is equally engaging, entertaining and exciting is a hard task to keep up with. So, it is best to combine both features if you want to be efficient with your time on the app. In that case, it is a good idea to come up with a schedule and frequency of the content you share. For example, Instagram stories can be shared on a daily basis while Reels can be shared once a week.

How to create Instagram Reels?

To create a new reel, tap the camera icon in the top left corner of your Instagram home feed. If Reels are available in your country, you will have the option to choose between Live, Story and Reels at the bottom of your screen. Then, all you have to do is start recording and editing your first reel.

How to use Instagram Reels?

With Instagram Reels, brands and Influencers have the opportunity to elevate their Instagram strategy. But how?

Share unique content. Create genuine and authentic content that aligns with your brand image and style. Emphasize on what makes you different and what makes you stand out from the crowd. Remember to have fun, be creative and show your personality.

Share behind-the-scenes content. Give exclusive access to your personal or professional life by creating exciting Reels that showcase your true colors. Share a story, show the process of making products, hype a new product launch or focus on your day-to-day activities. There is so much you can do!

Share informative and educational material. If you have no idea what to post on Reels, educational content is always an excellent way to gain more visibility on the app. By providing helpful information to your audience such as quick guides, "How Tos" and other tips, you will be able to attract people interested in what you have to say and therefore grow your following.

Share light-hearted content. All of us have seen short videos online that genuinely made us chuckle. Whether it is a cat video or something even more ridiculous, cheerful and snappy content often gets viral. So, if this is something that resonates with your brand or personality, focus on creating content that brings joy to your followers.

Start a new challenge or join an existing one. There is no denying that the Internet loves challenges. They are a great way to increase your followers in a short period of time. But not every challenge is a hit. Some are easily forgotten, while others just don't bring the hype. If you are unable to think of a challenge that you want to start, join an existing one. For example, one of the most random yet fascinating challenges of 2020 was the Fleetwood Mac challenge. A man named Nathan Apodaca went viral after he posted a video of himself riding his long board while lip-syncing a popular song and drinking a beverage. The challenge got so popular that many celebrities and Influencers joined by creating their own content. Even the original creators of the song jumped on the train. The song got millions of new views and streams and the beverage company won new customers. With that being said, challenges can be great if you catch the wave and show your creativity.

Lastly, make sure you have the Instagram basics covered to reach the most people:

- Choose an interesting cover image
- Think of a clever caption for your reel
- Include hashtags

BONUS

Engagement rate

There is more to Instagram than simply posting pictures, especially if you want to make money from your account. To do so, you need to know your analytics and measure them often because what gets measured, gets improved. Whether you are a brand, influencer, blogger or a personal profile, you need to be aware of how much your engagement matters. Having more engagement can bring your account to the Explore page, which will attract many eyeballs on your account. More people looking at your profile increases the chance of getting more followers and likes. If you are on the Explore page of Instagram, there is a big chance that you are also going to be at least on one of the Top posts from the hashtags you've added to a specific post. This will lead to even more exposure and followers.

But to get there, you have to play by Instagram rules and know one thing - even if the algorithm is always changing, the importance of the Instagram engagement rate stays the same. Having a good engagement rate will give you everything you need - from more followers, likes and comments to sponsorships and other unique opportunities.

What is Instagram engagement rate?

Engagement rate is the number you get after dividing the engagement you have (likes and comments) for a specific period of time to your followers. You can analyze your Engagement rate based on likes or comments, or both. You can even go crazier and analyze the engagement rate per every single post, it is up to you. To calculate the Engagement rate, the equations goes the following way:

Engagement rate = Engagement / Followers *

If you don't have the time to invest in calculating, you can use an engagement rate calculator, that will get you the same (or very similar) results. My favourite calculators to use are Phlanx and Triberr but you will find many engagement rate calculators on Google.

Once you get the results of how your posts are performing, you can conclude whether it is a good or a bad number. If you are experiencing an engagement rate below 1%, this is most likely not a good sign. If your engagement is between 1%-3% that would indicate that your account is having an average engagement rate. High engagement rate is considered having above 4% engagement. However, this does not apply to every Instagram account. Accounts with more followers, have less engagement rate. It is natural. Accounts with a bigger number of followers tend to have a lot of inactive people / ghost followers. So, it is impossible to compare the engagement of an Instagram account with 10 000 followers to the ones above 1 million because they are not in the same range.

To get a better picture where your account its standing, here is the industry standard:

   • Accounts below 1k followers MUST have at least 5-6% engagement rate
   • Accounts between 1k – 10k followers MUST have at least 3% engagement rate
   • Accounts between 10k - 100k followers MUST have at least 2.2% engagement rate
   • Accounts between 100k - 1M followers MUST have at least 2% engagement rate
   • Accounts above 10M followers MUST have at least 1.9% engagement

High Engagement rate

The algorithm takes account of how good your Instagram is performing based on your engagement rate (likes, comment, Saved posts and posts sent through DMs), and then decides the exposure your post will get. A high engagement rate indicates that most of your followers are engaging with your feed and enjoy the content you share. Having a good engagement rate will boost your account by giving it the exposure it needs. The more people like your content, the better Instagram will treat your account and the bigger the chance to get to the Explore page or Top posts of your hashtags, from where you can get a lot of exposure and traffic.

Note: Instagram Explore Page is different for everyone and it is based on the content you like, and content liked by the people you like. Getting on the Explore page can make your post viral, which will lead to a lot of opportunities, including hundreds of followers.

Quick Tip: Videos, who get to the Explore page can bring your account followers, likes and comments, over a week after posting your initial video post.

High engagement rate would also mean that there are people who look up to you. For personal profiles, high engagement rate is important when collaborating with brands. If they want you to promote their products, they would like to see an engaged community, who is more likely to buy their products.

For brands, high engagement rate indicates that your followers like your brand message. Engaged followers is how you build relationships that last. Brands with higher engagement rate are more trustworthy and have a better conversion rate of sales and leads. Plus, each time your followers interact with your content, the overall awareness of your brand is increased.

Low Engagement rate

A low engagement rate can mean a lot of things, but one for sure - your followers are not the biggest fan of your content. One of the top reasons why an engagement rate is low is because you have used one of the harmful methods to grow your account. Such as buying fake followers. If you have purchased bots, you shouldn't be surprised that they don't engage with your feed and stories.

Another reason might be if you have targeted the wrong group of people using the so famous follow/unfollow method. Or you have used the wrong set of hashtags. This is a very common mistake that can instantly decrease the engagement rate of your account.

It could also mean that the quality of the photos you are uploading are not as good as they have to be. High-quality content is crucial for success.

Or the reason for having a low engagement is because you are not posting at the right time of the day when most of your followers are active. This means that your post doesn't get the initial engagement (the engagement done in the first hour of posting) it needs which results in other posts getting your place under the "Top posts", making yours less visible.

If you are experiencing a low engagement rate and you want to improve it, don't worry - it is fixable, but you will have to work on it. The only exception is if you have bought followers, let's say 50 000 followers, then it is nearly impossible to rebuild your engagement rate as you will always have to divide it to these 50 000 plus the number of your real followers. But if that's not the case for you, here are some tips that could help you improve the engagement rate of your account:

1. Engage with others. You cannot force engagement from your followers. What you can do is try to connect with more people by liking and leaving genuine comments under their pictures. If you take your time to connect to people in your niche, then some of them might start engaging with you and as a bonus, some of their followers might become YOUR followers. If you have the time to answer the comments under your posts, do that as well. People like being appreciated and if you have a small amount of comments, you might as well reply to them.

2. Improve your photography skills/equipment. There is a very high chance that your followers are not liking your photos because they are low quality (blurry, positioned bad, bad filters etc.). To improve the quality of your pictures, the best thing you can do is to buy a DSLR but if you want to spend less money or none, you can use the camera on your phone. The trick of taking a good picture is the lighting of the photo. So, if you want to quickly improve, find the best location with natural light for your Instagram posts and learn the basics of using editing softwares, where you can play with brightness, exposure, contrast etc. (even Instagram offers editing tools that will instantly improve your pictures).

3. Try different demographics. What if you have less followers and likes because you are not targeting the right group of people?

In that case, you can do research on what type of people work best for your account. You can look at your competition and make an overall analysis on what type of people engage with them - males, females, what is the age gap, what are their interests and so on. If your account is Instagram business, you can look at your Insights which will give you some answers to what group of people is responding best to your content.

4. Post at the time when most of your followers are active & track your analytics. If you are serious about your Instagram account, it is very important to convert it to a professional account. For that, you will need to have a Facebook page and connect it to your IG account. Instagram Insights will give you information that you can only dream of. You will be able to see when your followers are most active, what their demographics are, how many reach and impressions your account has reached for the last week and more.

It will give you information about your stories, profile views, and where the likes on your posts came from. This will drastically improve the number of your likes which will increase your exposure and improve your engagement rate.

5. Work with others in your niche. Working with creators (with a number of followers similar to yours) can give you a lot of opportunities. You can get a slice of their followers, exchange some tips on how to grow in the industry, work on projects together and have some fun.

6. Find posts with the highest engagement rate and try to deliver more of that. People like some posts better than others. The key is to find which one of the posts they are interacting best with. Keeping a track of your engagement rate per post (in an excel sheet or word document) will show you which post is performing better than the others.

Every other method described in Part 2:Grow your profile will help your engagement rate because the only way to increase your engagement rate is by growing your account.

Part 3: Utilize the right strategy

This part of the book will focus on the strategy and why it's essential to have one. While the tricks for growth will give you an idea of what you should do with your account, having a Social Media Strategy will help you achieve your goal and get the most out of your account. As a brand owner, it might give you better results than expected because it will force you to answer questions to get a better understanding of how your business should adapt in the world of Social Media.

If you think you don't need to have a strategy, in order to succeed, you need to think twice! Even if this was possible before, there are millions daily active users, which means that the competition is way too big and you cannot count on luck anymore. Not having a goal and a strategy built around that goal is one of the most common mistakes that stop your account from growing. So, take a deep breath and let's look at how to build your strategy as a brand and personal profile.

As a brand

Finding and utilizing the best strategy for your business is not as simple because there are many variables to consider. To begin with, you have to focus on a few different categories - your ideal customer, audience, goals and plan that you have for growing your account. You will need to answer questions like:

- ➤ What is your ideal client - age, location, degree (the demographics of your dream client)?
- ➤ Where can you find your audience - some might be big fans of Reddit, others might prefer Quora or forums?
- ➤ When do they go online? (You can track this with Instagram Insights if you have an Instagram Business account)
- ➤ What traits or interests do they have with one another?

- ➢ What is the goal you want to achieve with the strategy - increase sales, more brand awareness, get website traffic?
- ➢ Which one of the methods from Part Two of this book are you going to use to get the most results - are you going to focus on giveaways or perhaps using the geotag for local awareness?
- ➢ When and how often are you going to post?
- ➢ What type of content would be the perfect fit for your audience?
- ➢ How is it different from your competition?
- ➢ What is the unique thing about your brand that encourages people to follow you?

Before you build your strategy and use all methods for growth, you need to know the answers to these questions. Once you know the goal you want to achieve, then and only then think of what type of strategy you are going to utilize. To do that, you need to have a clear vision about the following three components:

1. Content Marketing
2. Planning your content
3. Segmented Hashtags

Content Marketing (Brands)

The content you post is the core of your Instagram. If your posts aren't good, then it is nearly impossible to grow and be successful on the platform. There are four types of content strategy that you can use - products, company's culture, a mix of both - products & culture and user-generated content. Here is how they differ from one another:

Products

Sharing products on Instagram is a well-known technique for increasing sales. It is used by brands and retailers around the globe because it is an easy and efficient way to display your products and if you have the right audience, every post can turn into a closed deal. It can boost your brand awareness, increase traffic and hype your audiences for the launch of your new products. More interests will generate more sales once the product is out.

Creating a feed solely focused on your products is not an easy task. It requires a lot of work, creativity and originality. A great example of this type of content strategy on Instagram is **EOSproducts**.

Example of an Instagram feed with Products in the cosmetic industry:

Company's Culture

If you are an organization and you need brand awareness, sharing culture-centric pictures can be the way to go. This is an excellent way to share the core values of your business and express humanity by establishing a clear vision of what your company stands for across all different areas of the organization.

Company culture is what binds your organization together. It can differ from telling a story in your posts to emphasizing on the culture that is associated with your brand. It is how you give your brand an identity and show the world what values your brand has especially if your customers share them too. A great example of this type of content strategy on Instagram is **Hootsuite**.

Products + Culture

Just because you are selling products or you offer services, doesn't mean that you have to ignore the community part of your brand. Combining product/services with culture content can give you amazing results because it can make your community stronger and your brand more reputable. You can use this strategy to provide bigger value to your followers by sharing informative tips and entertaining content that align with your culture side while you also promote your products/services. A great example of this type of content strategy on Instagram is **Buffer**.

Example of an Instagram feed with Products/Services & Culture of a beauty salon:

User-generated content (UGC)

If you have been on the market for a very long time, then you must have loyal customers. And when people love your products, they will share it with the world. If they create high-quality posts of your products with nice captions, you as a brand can simply reshare the best of them. Reposting their pictures will show your followers that you care. Not only that, it will show that you have a group of loyal customers, so you must be doing something right. A great example of this type of content strategy on Instagram is **Tentsile**.

Planning content

Although there are only four types of content strategy you can use for your Instagram account, it is best to choose the one that describes your brand and purpose the most. The strategy you choose must be aligned with your brands' target audience and core values.

However, be reasonable with your choices. If you choose to focus solely on products, make sure you can provide enough HQ content material and you won't run out of content ideas. If you are unable to do so, combine product &

culture content instead. If you want to use Instagram as a showcase for your organization, focus on culture content strategy. If your main goal is to build trust and form a community on Social Media, UGC can be the most beneficial strategy for you.

The best way to move forward with your account is to create content for at least one week in advance and schedule through different online platforms like Buffer and Hootsuite. You will need to carefully combine the different types of content you create with the strategy you are utilizing.

Segmented hashtags

The last part of your strategy is to use segmented hashtags for your posts. As you should already know by now, choosing only the hashtags relevant to your profile is a MUST. Especially for a new profile - there is no other efficient way for your target group to discover you.

As a personal profile

To create an efficient strategy, you need three major components - your target group, a goal for your account and analytics. You will need to answer the following questions:

- ➢ What's your target group - who are the people interested in your content?
- ➢ What's your goal - what do you want to achieve with your account?
- ➢ Are your target group helping you to achieve your goals (analytics can answer this one for you)?
- ➢ Who is your competition - what makes you different?

When you have the answers to these questions, you will be able to determine the best objective for your profile and the most suitable growing techniques. Set a goal you want to achieve and divide it into smaller milestones. For example, if your goal is to get to 10 000 followers, set your first milestone to 1000 followers. This way, you will not stress about how to get to this big number but instead you will focus on finding what works best for your account growth.

Quick Tip: If you have no idea which growth method will get your account to 1000 followers, here is a suggestion based on Part 2: Grow your profile of this book - start with hashtags and engage with others. Then, slowly expand the methods you are using. Add Instagram stories to your strategy while you also cross-promote your account on other platforms like Pinterest, Facebook and Reddit. Once you hit 1000 followers, organize a small giveaway for your current audience.

Take it step by step because the way you grow rapidly changes when you get to the big followers. But if you rush it or you don't pay attention to what's working, you will get overwhelmed when more people come your way. Not to mention if your posts are not getting enough engagement.

No matter what type of account you are running, you need to take your time and focus on your goal. Not having one or having way too many won't get you anywhere as you won't be able to focus on one thing.

Instagram is a platform that focuses on visuals and people love that. So, you need to know how your account is different from your competition and use it as your advantage. But at the same time you need to blend in, in order to stand out. It is like that because all of the accounts with thousands of followers have the same exact thing in common – high-quality content.

Quick Tip: One thing you should avoid at all cost is posting duplicate content. There is no excuse to post the same picture over and over again. Don't be lazy because people will notice. This is one of the biggest push offs that you can do.

Having a strategy will keep you on the right track and will help you stay focused on the end goal. The process of finding a strategy that works best for your profile will help you learn new things about your business and your followers. It is no longer enough to just post and hope for followers. You, as a business or a personal profile, need to connect with your group of followers, build a community and the opportunities will come soon after.

Part 3: Utilize the right strategy - How does the Instagram algorithm work?

The Instagram algorithm has been a hot topic of discussion ever since the platform changed the way they show content to the users back in 2016. Before that time, Instagram users had the option to view their news feed in reverse-chronological order. But this is not the case anymore. And as algorithms evolve, many marketing tips and tricks that worked yesterday do not work in present times.

Today, the Instagram algorithm is much more advanced and relies on multiple factors. Such algorithms often decide when and who sees the content you share and shows the most relevant content for you on your feed, Instagram stories, IGTV and Reels. Understanding how it works is essential for every account determined to find success on the platform.

How does the Instagram algorithm work in 2021?

The algorithm shows your new post to a small group of your followers. Then, it measures how fast and how many of your followers engage with your new post. After that, it compares the engagement received on your recent post to the engagement of your past posts - the better the engagement on your recent post, the higher the reach you will get and the higher the chance of making it to the Explore page on Instagram.

Which factors affect the Instagram algorithm?

Everything you see on your Instagram feed is a combination of all of your behaviours on the platform. This includes the accounts you interact with the most, accounts you follow and similar posts to the ones you have engaged with before (liked/commented on).

Instagram Algorithm - Your Feed

#1 Interest. The Instagram algorithm is based on accounts that users explore on Instagram and similar types of content that they interact with. If Instagram users have enjoyed certain types of posts in the past, the algorithm will make sure to show them similar posts in the future. In addition, the more the algorithm thinks you will like a specific type of content, the higher the changes for it to appear in your Instagram feed.

#2 Relationships. The Instagram algorithm focuses on content from accounts that you interact with and care about. User engagement in the form of likes, follow, comments and shares/DMs are also important indicators for content users might enjoy. That's one of the reasons why Instagram will show you posts from someone you have just followed in your feed - it tries to calculate the interest level between the two accounts.

The algorithm also pays attention to the following interactions:

- People you send a Direct Message to
- People you search for
- People you tag

The algorithms also prioritize content with a high engagement rate. However, the most important engagement options for feed raking are:

- For image content - comments, likes, reshares
- For video content - comment, views, likes, reshares

So, it is not about how many followers one account has. It is about the connections you make and the content you create.

#3 Post Time. The moment your content was first published is yet another important thing that the Instagram algorithm takes into consideration.

Instagram wants to show the latest and most exciting posts to their users, which means that newer posts have a higher chance of reaching more people compared to posts that are on the platform for a long period of time. This is one of the reasons why consistency is key.

#4 Other factors from a user point of view. The way Instagram users spend their time on the platform is also important for the Instagram algorithm. The algorithm will show the most popular and top performing posts since the last time the user opened the app.

- Frequency. If you spend a decent amount of time on Instagram every day, your feed will have a more chronological look. You will still see the top-performing content but you will also see more posts including underperforming ones. When there are no new posts to discover, Instagram will show you suggested posts based on your interests and the content you enjoyed in the past. If you visit the platform less often, Instagram will show you the highlights of the day. Your feed will be sorted into posts that the algorithm thinks you will like instead of following a chronological order.

- Follower count. Instagram followers are a small piece of the puzzle for success. Although the follower count is not as important as the rest factors, the number of people you follow as well as the number of followers these people have can play a role for the content you see in your Instagram feed. For example, if you follow celebrities who have a lot of followers and decent post engagement, you are more likely to see their recent posts compared to accounts you have less followers and you rarely interact with. Similar to that, if you follow thousands of people, Instagram will not show you every post but sort out the most relevant to you.

So, if users follow a lot of Instagram accounts, there is a lot of competition for the top spot in their news feed. On the contrary, if users are not that active on the platform, brands and Influencers decrease the chance of having their content seen even if it is not in the top spot in their feed. This information can be used by personal profiles and businesses to improve their content marketing strategy and tailor to their audience.

Instagram Algorithm - The Explore Page

The Explore page of Instagram is famous for discovering new content similar
to what you already like. So, you will not be surprised to find out that the
Instagram algorithm delivers content to users' Explore page based on past
behaviour and content interactions. The Explore page is personalized to show
relevant and popular content based on every individuals' interests, similar to
your Instagram feed. But unlike the content you see in your feed, the posts on
the Explore page are from new accounts that you are not following.

Instagram Algorithm - Instagram stories, IGTV & Reels

The way the Instagram algorithm shows stories and video content such as
IGTV and Reels is similar to the way it shows content in your feed. It
prioritizes accounts that you engage with the most while it also takes into
consideration the timeliness of the story (when it was posted). Newer stories,
Reels and IGTV posts from accounts you engage with on a regular basis -
whether it is through DMs, likes, comments, story reactions or story views -
will appear first in your feed.

It is important to understand how the algorithm works in order to take full
advantage of the opportunity that Instagram has to offer. For example, from
everything mentioned above, it is safe to assume that if you want to reach
more people, you need to post at the time your audience is most active. This
will show your post to more people and increase the chances of getting more
likes, comments, followers, saves and shares. However, the algorithm is
always changing. So, make sure to pay attention to what works best for your
channel and be open to changes.

Part 3: Utilize the right strategy - How to plan content for your Instagram account?

One of the greatest challenges for businesses and influencers on Social Media is creating meaningful, relevant and interesting content that resonates with their audience. Whether it is entertaining, educational or inspirational material, it is not always an easy task to come up with engaging posts.

You have probably heard the phrase 'Content is King' a million times. Content creation is important on any Social platform because it can make your page very successful. The content you create should resemble your personality, voice and style.

But If you have been long enough on the platform, you probably understand how difficult of a task it is to create good content on a regular basis. Without a proper plan and tools, content creation becomes impossible after a certain period of time. And it is exhausting not to say the least. That's why it is crucial to have a way to discover content when you are stuck or run out of ideas.

How to plan content for your Instagram account?

If you have no idea what to post next on your channel, consider establishing content pillars for your online presence.

Content Pillars

Content pillars, also called content buckets, are a set of 2-6 topics, directly related to your niche. They can be helpful when it comes to creating consistent content, getting clarity on your niche and growing your audience at a faster rate.

To get a better understanding of what a content pillar is, think of it as one big informative piece of content on a specific topic that can be broken into many smaller pieces and used as content material for your Instagram page. Content pillars can be blog articles, eBooks, reports, guides, videos. They are topics that resonate with your target audience. That's why understanding who is your target is very important.

Content pillars can be used as a strategic tool to discover content for your account and help you plan and create months of content in advance. However, they are not a replacement for your niche or theme but rather a helpful way to draw out all the different angles of content that's interesting for your audience.

For example, if I had an Instagram account focused on Instagram Marketing and growth, this book would be an excellent content pillar because I can use it to share a lot of insights and relevant material that people in my niche would definitely want to learn more about.

Or, if I had a beauty account, the content creator's pillars could be positive mindset, beauty secrets and tips, self-love, makeup trends, etc.

How to apply content pillars to your account?

The easiest way to start is by analyzing the main thematic pillars for your Instagram account by creating a few large pieces of bedrock content.

What is bedrock content?

Bedrock content is a piece of content that acts like the core of your content marketing strategy. It gives your content a clear marketing goal and purpose. Bedrock content is directly related to content pillars. Think of it as one big piece of information that can be divided into a few smaller pieces of valuable insights (content pillars).

Bedrock content should be:

- Interesting enough to encourage people to take the next step and act.
- Engaging enough to make people curious about what you do
- Relevant enough to never go out of fashion
- Insightful enough to never run out of content ideas

Content Calendar

Content pillars will help you find new ideas of what to post next but a content calendar will make sure you have a plan for your Instagram channel. Planning your posts and stories in advance with the help of a content calendar will help you with the challenge of creating content.

What is a content calendar?

A content calendar allows brands and personal profiles to plan and create strategic content in advance, designed to hit specific goals and reach a specific group of people. It reduces the pressure of posting every day and it also reduces the time you spend on creating content. It is beneficial for Instagram users to have a content calendar because it removes the stress of coming up with different content every day.

With the help of a content calendar, you will be able to visualize your future content and make it compatible with your Social Media strategy. If your account is not performing well over time, the content calendar will help you to identify the reason for that. In addition, you can use it to create content for multiple Social Media platforms. This will help you to stay organized and use the same voice across all Social Media channels. And that's a big plus!

How to start using a content calendar?

You can find a content calendar template online but you can also create one with the help of a spreadsheet app. A content calendar usually includes the type of the post you want to share, description (caption) details, hashtag selection and a lot of space for analytics.

For the best results, start your content calendar by planning out content for at least one month in advance. This will help you prepare for important dates and events such as the upcoming holiday season or Valentines day. Content calendar will help you analyze if you are striking the right balance of your content pillars.

When your content for the month is ready, all you need to do is transfer the information from your content calendar to a planning app (such as Hootsuite, Buffer, Later) that allows you to upload and schedule multiple Instagram posts.

Once the month is over and the content calendar is fully filled, it becomes an archive. You can use it to track your progress and reflect on your Instagram channel. It is your job to use it to examine what works best and has the highest engagement for the previous month. With the help of a content calendar, you can answer questions like – did we achieve our goals? How many new followers did we gain? Which is the top performing post of the month based on likes/reach/comments/followers gained?

Quick Tip: Combine your content calendar with analytic tools to get the best overview of your account. Tools, such as Instagram Insights will give you more information and accurate numbers, so you can easily track your account's progress.

The content calendar will not grow your Social Media accounts. At least not directly. But it will teach you to plan ahead and be organized. And those are two very valuable skills you must master if you want to manage one or many Social Media accounts and make a living out of it.

In addition, having a content calendar will help you learn to be consistent and create strategic content for your Social Media accounts. You will never run out of ideas because you won't have the pressure of posting every day. But most importantly, with a content calendar, you will be able to see what your target group finds appealing.

Content Suggestions

If you have no idea what to post online, here are some suggestions to help you get started:

20 Post topics for brands:

1. Share your company's background story
2. Share milestones celebration & awards
3. Introduce the team
4. Share your industry knowledge
5. Host a contest/giveaway
6. Start a challenge
7. Share an exclusive offer
8. Share user-generated content
9. Share customer testimonials
10. Share a palate cleanser - something funny & cute
11. Share industry statistics
12. Start a conversation
13. Share company news & updates
14. Run a poll
15. Highlight a recent event
16. Share an inspirational quote
17. Tease new products
18. Ask for feedback
19. Share an industry fact/myth
20. Promote your website

20 Post topics for personal profiles:

1. Promote your blog post
2. Share engaging stock images
3. Shout out another creator

4. Share your hobbies

5. Do a #AskMeAnything post

6. Share DIY Tips and Tricks

7. Leverage quotes

8. Share exciting news

9. Organize a giveaway

10. Join/Start a challenge

11. Share a throwback photo

12. Share related memes

13. Create seasonal posts

14. Highlight your favorite spot/coffee shop

15. Share a positive message

16. Tell a story

17. Share your accomplishments

18. Cover an event

19. Share education content (tutorials)

20. Team up with other creators and share the posts on your feed

Part 3: Utilize the right strategy - How to create viral material on Instagram in 2021?

With over 1 billion monthly users already on the app, Instagram is crowded with start-ups and Influencers competing for the attention of the regular user. While some focus on slow and steady growth, others chase the 'viral' moment of their career. I am sure you have heard this word to a point that it sounds cliche and obnoxious, but what does it mean to 'go viral'?

When I think of viral content, I envision snappy, interesting, attention-grabbing material that you can watch over and over again. It is the type of content that makes you want to share with your friends and/or save it for later. Viral content gets significantly more engagement on Instagram than your regular posts usually do - you know you have a viral post when it has thousands of likes/comments and millions of views. The more recognition your content receives, the more exposure your Instagram profile will get.

The perks of creating viral content

Creating content that is loved by many is a very hard task. But it comes with a few great perks for your Instagram account:

Free Exposure. Creating shareable content will bring a huge new wave of people to your Instagram page. This is a great opportunity for brands to gain more popularity and increase brand awareness. Similar to businesses, personal profiles can also use viral content to increase their visibility and put their name out there for the world to know.

New financial opportunities. With your posts being shared, tagged and sent over DMs, you will have the chance to monetize the traffic you are bringing. Brands can use this to promote products and increase their revenue while personal profiles can capitalize by getting big endorsements from brands they love or by promoting their own merchandise.

Growth. A content piece, shared by millions of people on the Internet is one sure way to experience fast growth on the app. Creating viral material gives brands and personal profiles access to a new audience. It will bring new engagement to your old posts, thousands of new followers and a lot of new connections.

How to create viral content on Instagram?

Going viral is one of the best ways possible to grow your Instagram following. But it is an extremely difficult task. Many people join the platform with the only intent to go viral. While this is exciting and it can bring a lot of attention to your Instagram, it is very important to understand the reason why you want to go viral. What do you want to achieve? Are you interested in getting a lot of followers? Or are you planning on monetizing your content as soon as possible? Or maybe both?

Whatever the reason might be, you need to have a clear goal of what you want to achieve and the number that you want to reach to consider your content 'viral'. Some believe that 100 000 views is enough while I might argue that at least a few million views are necessary to truly feel the change.

There are no general rules as to what makes your content go viral. Many companies and Influencers spend months, even years, establishing patterns by analyzing their audience, posts performance and profile analytics before they reach their first viral online moment. Sometimes, a post gets viral because of the uniqueness of its nature. Rarely, a post will get viral because of luck and great timing.

With all that being said, 'going viral' is a rare occurrence. It does not take one day to get there. In fact, it can take years to get a viral post with millions of views but it can also never happen at all. And this is okay. Because there are one billion other people competing with you.

However, there are some similarities when it comes to the content that gets 'viral'. My own experience has shown me that if you want to create viral material, your content needs to get on the Explore page on Instagram of as many people as possible.

The elements of viral content

High engagement rate and great visuals of the post itself are amongst the most important criteria for creating viral material. High engagement rate is the key to getting on the Explore page of Instagram. But the Instagram algorithm will not favor your post if it is blurry or low quality.

Creating authentic and genuine content is also important. The posts you share should not feel staged or promotional. Quite the opposite! Your goal is to create a content piece that is sharable, snappy, captivating and unexpected.

Another piece of the puzzle of creating viral content is consistency. Patience and persistence are important traits to help you stay focused on your goals. There will be times when you will create awesome content that will not get the recognition it deserves. But that does not mean that the post is bad. Maybe it is bad timing or the wrong target audience. Whatever the reason might be, make sure to identify the problem that is holding your post back so you can prevent it for your future content.

The use of relevant hashtags is yet another element of creating viral content. Hashtags can be used to increase the engagement rate of your post as well as to reach the right group of people in your niche.

Tips to create your first viral post

If you have all the elements mentioned above, you have a higher chance to go viral but there is still no guarantee that this will happen. Creating viral material takes time and requires the right Marketing strategy. But there are some tips to help you get started:

Use current events. Create content around a relevant hot topic that people are already talking about. Use a trending event that you can somehow connect to what you do. For example, one of my best content pieces this year was a video of my cat trying to get my attention while I am trying to do my work. This narrative fits perfectly with the working from home topic that many experienced in 2020. Although my original post was created in the autumn of 2019 before remote working was even a thing, it got over 100 000 views until the beginning of 2020 when it was reposted by some bigger channels including 9GAG, which brought millions of new views.

Take your audience on an emotional journey. We are creatures of emotion. That's why the one thing that most viral content has in common is provoking emotion in the user. Whether it is sadness, happiness, motivation or inspiration, think about the emotion you want your profile to portray. Use it to tell a story that resonates with your brand and it is meaningful to your target demographics.

Know your industry and audience. Keep on eye on the latest trends and news in your industry and use it to create content that your audience craves. Discuss relevant topics in a new light or share unique ideas that change the way your followers think about a current event.

Research what works. Studying your niche will make it easier to create better content for your Instagram channel. That does not mean to copy whatever your competitors might be doing. Research your niche and try to spot similarities between the most viral material in recent months/years. Take notes of the trending posts you see on the Explore page and use this information to come up with posts you know your audience will respond best to.

Get controversial. Controversy works. Today, more than ever, too many people get their '15 seconds of fame' because they appear controversial. Going against the grain is an easy way to get spotted but it is not always the most effective one (although I am sure PR teams would disagree). If you share a different opinion and you genuinely think going against the grain is suitable for your online personality or brand, then just go for it. While some might disagree with you, others, who share your opinion will applaud you for the courage and appreciate you for your strong beliefs. This does not mean to attack someone's character or background.

Be unique. Contrary to using trending events, you can also go viral by being unique and innovative with the help of your own creativity and imagination. If you have a charming personality or you appeal to certain demographics or a particular niche, use this to get your viral moment.

Use videos. It is a known fact that videos perform significantly better on Instagram compared to images. Short and exciting video content has the potential to be seen by millions of people. But it has to be creative, unique and intriguing.

There is no formula for creating viral material because you can never predict the next big thing. You can measure the performance of your posts and assume how your future content will perform but it is still uncertain because creating viral content is an exception rather than a rule.

If your goal is to get millions of views, work in this direction but do not stress too much about it. There are one billion people using the app and at least half of them are trying to get the free exposure. And while the results might be worth it, it is still reasonable to ask yourself the following question - is the content you share attracting the right group of people?

Remember, you might get millions of views and still sell no products. Because when it comes to your business or influence, it is crucial to focus on the people who will actually buy what you have to offer - your audience.

Part 3: Utilize the right strategy - Followers > Following

When your Instagram profile gets to the point, when you gain followers every day, you might feel the urge to return the favor and follow the accounts that have just followed you. Of course, some of them would be worth following because of their good content or just because you are interested in building a relationship with them. However, know one thing - just because people are voluntarily following you does not mean that they expect the same in return. And the group of people who expect such things will unfollow you either way because they are playing the follow for follow game. With time, you will discover that there are a lot of people interested in your content who would hit the follow button because they want to learn more about you.

One of the strategies that you need to implement regardless of the type of your account is to never have more people under the following tab compared to your followers' tab. You want to have an aesthetic look and clear account, because this is how you will attract more followers in the long-run and find brands to collaborate with / attract clients. Plus, you want to grow the number of your followers, not how many people you are following. If that isn't convincing enough, Instagram allows you to follow only 7 500 followers per account. So, the space for your following is limited and you don't want to spend it on any other person, with whom you have nothing in common. You are risking to make your Instagram news feed full of low-quality photos that you won't comment on nor you want to have anything with them.

Note: There is a huge difference between an account with 1000 followers and 1000 following and an account with 13 000 followers and 1 000 following. You can tell if the other account is follow for follow. However, don't be mistaken that the account with 13 000 followers has only organic followers, he might have bought his account or paid for a number. The easiest way to tell is by looking at the accounts engagement rate. If you don't have time to deal with that, you can simply look at the number of likes. For example, if the account who has 13 000 followers has only 20 - 100 likes, it means that something isn't right. And that is pretty visible nowadays because so many people know about the follow/unfollow trick.

Part 3: Utilize the right strategy

Most of the time posting high-quality pictures is only half of the job. Having a nice feed will get you followers, but if you want to maximize your engagement, you will need to master the art of captions.

The caption is the text you write under your photo. It is limited to 2200 characters, but the first 100 characters are the most important. Captions can be used to close the deal because they are the ones encouraging people to purchase your products. They can be the reason why brands contact you or customers buy from you. Every Social platform requires captions as they can be the one convincing your potential followers that you are worth the follow.

To create an engaging caption you will need to spend some minutes and focus on the first sentence - these 100 chapters that will draw attention to the rest of the text. If you are a brand that promotes a new product never start with the features and advantages of this particular product. This type of post is called a right hook. Your aim is to sell your product by telling a story or a catchy phrase relatable to your followers. It shouldn't be long but it should be something that people can connect to. Because if you grab their attention with something relatable, they will keep reading. And that's where you add the product description. That's how you "hook" them.

You can research inspirational quotes and write them in your caption. People love this. You can also be funny and entertain your followers. But don't forget one thing. Have a clear CTA (Call To Action) message. Whether you are a brand or a personal profile, a CTA can encourage people to like your post, follow your profile, click your link in the biography, sell your products and increase engagement.

It is also a very good practice to divide your captions from your hashtags. You can use a space bar or dots. But don't add them to your comments. Many people claim that this method works, but for how much longer will it work?

A very long time ago, when Instagram was still new on the market, there were no limits on how many people you can follow. But once people started abusing their rights, Instagram limited the number to 7 500 followers per account. Later, people started spamming likes and comments and the platform had to once again change the way their algorithm works. Now, there are restrictions which if you violate, you can get a temporary or a permanent ban from the platform. All that shows that Instagram is constantly changing. Because there are so many people abusing the system once again by adding additional hashtags in the comment section (plus the one on their post) it might not last too long.

People use captions to leave their message, tell their stories, inspire and share their everyday life. So, the next time you want to post something, think about the caption and the people who are about to receive your message. Write it as a draft and improve it until you are satisfied with it.

Part 3: Utilize the right strategy - Instagram Guides

Instagram Guides is a new Instagram feature that allows users to curate, pair and share tips, news and other relevant resources with their audience. It was initially introduced to spread helpful information during the pandemic and for this reason, it was limited to the health and wellness industry. However, Instagram gave everyone the chance to create their own Guides at the end of 2020.

Guides can be used by Instagram creators and businesses as a new way to share long-form content with their audience. Instagram users can use the feature to curate tips, commentary, tutorials or advice from your own Instagram feed or other creators on the platform and categorize it in a new tab that can be found on their Instagram profile

The feature is very similar to a blog post because it encourages users to spend more time on the app compared to a typical post in the story or feed.

How to create your first Instagram Guide?

1. Go to your Instagram profile
2. Click the plus (+) button in the upper right corner of your screen
3. From the 'Create New' pop up select 'Guide'
4. Choose the type of the guide you want to create:
    1. Places
    2. Products
    3. Posts
5. Once you have collected the posts you want, add a title and select a cover photo for your Guide
6. Add a description of your Guide which you can find below the cover photo.
7. Add titles and descriptions for all of the posts you have curated

8. Click 'Next'
9. You can click on 'Share', it will add your new guide to your Instagram feed immediately but you can also 'Save as a Draft' for later
10.   Once your Guide is posted, you can promote it to your Story and Dms

How to use Instagram Guides?

Places. This option will allow you to choose from a location listed on Instagram - you can search for a specific location of your choice, use the location of your previous posts or choose a place you Saved. You can add up to five posts from the content related to that location. Select the location/place you want to add to your guide.

This option is an amazing opportunity for local businesses with a physical location to highlight user-generated content to increase the local reach of their business.

Influencers can also benefit from this new feature - they use Places Guides to share their favorite restaurant,coffee shop, nail salon or rank their favorite travel destinations.

Products. Product Guides let users add their favorite items in one place. In order to find the product they are looking for, users have to select the brand first before they can access the products. Instagram users have the ability to choose products from popular brands or directly from their Wishlist section.

Products Guide is another feature that can be used by brands and Influencers for the same reason - to promote their products. You can choose to add guides based on your products' category, color, theme or you can use one product guide to showcase only one item with multiple photos.

Posts. My favorite option from the three is posts guides because it allows users to curate information from their own Instagram content but also from the posts they have saved before (the ones from your Saved tab). You can choose up to 30 posts to share to a single guide.

Brands and personal profiles can use posts guides to get creative and provide value to their audience. With posts guides, Instagram users can curate educational material such as tips, industry secrets and tutorials.

Part 3: Utilize the right strategy - Instagram for SEO?

If you search on Google the name of a celebrity or any public figure (vlogger, writer, entertainer, musician) with Social Media accounts, you will find their Instagram, Twitter and other SM channels on the very first page of the search results. That's where Social Media and SEO interconnect.

Search Engine Optimization (SEO) is the process of optimizing your content in order to rank higher on Google and other search engines with an effort to get more website traffic from search engine's organic search results. With simple words, it is the process of optimizing your content in order to 'translate' it to the search engines like Google and Bing.

SEO can be very beneficial for self-branding and businesses. The reason why SEO is so unique is that it brings organic free traffic to your website. And this is valuable. There is much to talk about when it comes to SEO, but what is the relationship between SEO and Social Media?

The answer is one simple word - content. Both Social Media and SEO are very dependent on high-quality content. Whether it is a book, a video or a blog post, Social Media is the best place to promote your content. SEO, on the other hand, ensures that your activity online improves your search engine ranking.

How to use Instagram to rank first on Google and other search engines?

ALT TEXT

A feature Instagram released in 2019 is alt text for your posts. If you have ever worked on a website, you probably know that alt text can be a very important tool for SEO strategy. Alternative text, alt text for short, is designed to help visually impaired users to enjoy their Instagram experience but it can be used as a powerful SEO tool as well.

Instagram alt text feature allows users to write captions for their photos. Because of alt text, your content can appear in search results in Google, Bing and other search engines. It can help your posts to rank better in the algorithm and have your results pulled for voice search.

Instagram adds an automatic alt text of your posts. But if you want to do it manually, you can access the alt text option available in Advanced Settings, which you can find below the options to share your content to other Social Media channels right before sharing your new post.

Optimize your Instagram profile

Think of Instagram as one big visual engine. But instead of search terms, Instagram uses hashtags and locations to categorize its content. In order to show up for the correct term in the search bar, Instagram uses information such as your username, profile name, and biography to show the most accurate results.

If you want to be at the top of the search, you will need to work within the app to do so.

The first step you would want to take is to optimize your Instagram profile. This is an important step that will give an overall boost to your Instagram account in the long-run. If you don't optimize your profile, you won't benefit from the traffic you get on your Instagram page.

Although the optimization process is very simple, here are some basic rules that you might find useful:

1. Make sure your Instagram profile is set to public instead of private.
2. Use a recognizable and easily searchable Instagram username that connects to your brand.

3. Convert to a Professional account

Let's talk more about your Instagram name - username and profile name.
You would want to have the same username for all Social Media channels.

Instagram username is what makes your profile unique (it can't have two
identical names) and it is the name you see when someone tags your account
(i.e. @instagram). Your username is a primary keyword. Keywords are short
key phrases that are relevant to your brand message and niche. For example,
your company name or something connected to your industry, specialty or
passion can be the perfect username. It is what describes your business the
best. Although you can change it, you would prefer to keep the same
username because this is what will rank higher on Google and Instagram.

Instagram profile name is not as unique and you can find it under your profile
photo on your Instagram profile. Even though your profile name is not as
important as the username, it is another thing that can be optimized to rank
higher on Google and Instagram. However, unlike the username, your profile
name is a secondary keyword. And while the primary keyword is what
defines you and your business, secondary keywords are what describes it
better. For example, if your primary keyword is 'coffee shop', secondary
keywords might be considered 'espresso', 'beverages', 'frappe', etc.

So even if someone is not looking for your primary keyword, you still have a
chance to be found in the search results by other users as you match the
user's search.

The same way you optimize your Instagram username and profile name, you
should do for your biography description (bio) and Instagram content.
Instagram is a self-contained search engine, so everything you do should be
focused on finding the right keywords that work best for your business.
Whether it is the caption of your post, your hashtag set or bio description,
relevant keywords are needed to index your account to a relevant category
and help you show up in search results. And remember - optimizing your
content is an ongoing task.

Track your analytics

Social Media Marketing is all about telling a story with the help of a compelling image, relevant text, and hashtags, but it would be nothing without analytics. The same applies to SEO. Although SEO is a slow process, you should keep an eye on how your SEO techniques are impacting your overall Social Media goals, the moment you start optimizing your Instagram profile. It can take a while before you are able to see your Instagram account on the first page on Google.

SEO is a long-term strategy and it can be extremely frustrating when you don't see instant results. Although Google hasn't confirmed that Social Media has a direct effect on SEO ranking if you optimize your Instagram account, you will be able to rank your Instagram account on the first page on Google in less than 6 months. If you use ALT text some of your content can rank as well.

These are some basic tips that will help you get better exposure on both Instagram search and other search engines. So when you monetize your Instagram profile, you will already have organic traffic coming to your website.

Part 3: Utilize the right strategy - Instagram Milestones

If you have no idea what to do with your Instagram strategy, you can prioritize increasing the number of your followers by dividing your goals to four different but equally important milestones. Focusing on these steps will boost your profile and allow you to taste the sweet life of Instagram.

Instagram Milestone #1 - Reach 100 followers

If you are serious about your Instagram account and you want to grow and earn money, the very first step is to convert it to a Professional account. This will give you access to Instagram Insights where you can learn more information about your Instagram profile such as your best performing content (posts and stories), activity (reach and impressions) and audience. However, before you reach 100 followers, some of this information will not be available to your account. For example, you would not be able to see when your followers are most active throughout the days. This will stop you from posting at the best time, when most of your followers are active.

Instagram Milestone #2 - Reach 500 followers

Once you hit 500 followers on Instagram, you would be able to properly use a very important feature that would help you grow your profile - hashtags in Instagram stories. And just like a regular post, using relevant hashtags in your stories will increase your exposure and your story will reach hundreds, if not thousands of people (depending on the volume of the hashtag and the relevancy of your story). All of them would be potential followers as they are probably interested in this specific topic. If your story is of great quality and you also have a nice feed and a catchy biography, a big number of these viewers can become your new followers.

Instagram Milestone #3 - Reach 1000 followers

Although you don't unlock a specific feature from reaching 1000 followers, this milestone is a very important step to your progress. Why 1000 followers?

To get so many people interested in your profile, is not an easy task. Because you do not know what's working for your niche and Instagram account. But if you are able to get 1000 people interested in your profile, then you can also get 2 times more, 10 times more, 100 times more and so on. You will know what steps to follow and what works for your profile and you would be able to multiply it.

Instagram Milestone #4 - Get to 10 000 followers

To reach 10 000 followers and get the Swipe Up option to your stories, you will need to know that this is not a short-term task. Unlike the previous three important milestones, getting 10 000 followers on Instagram requires time, dedication and utilizing the right methods for your account. This is the most obvious Instagram milestone you WANT to achieve because once you hit 10 000 followers, you will be able to add links to your stories. And that's a huge deal.

With one swipe up, your audience will be able to look at your website, shop, blog without leaving Instagram. You can add any (appropriate) link, hype your audience with new products, announce giveaways and so much more. Once your story is up, you can track how many people visited the link from your Instagram story, using story Insights.

Part 3: Utilize the right strategy - Important Instagram Metrics

Instagram offers analytics (Instagram Insights) to get more detailed information about your content and audience. Understanding Instagram Insights is an important process of your Instagram journey. You can use your findings to optimize your Instagram strategy, learn more about the content preferences of your audience and increase the number of your followers. But to do so, you need to know where to look at and what to measure.

What are the most important Instagram metrics?

Instagram Growth Metric. This is one of the most important metrics you need to keep an eye on. With the Instagram Growth metric, you can identify the peaks and lows of your Instagram accounts when it comes to the number of followers gained for a specific period of time. This metric will help you understand which content brings the most engagement and followers to your Instagram account. You can use it to establish a pattern and understand what your audience likes to see the most from your content.

To get access to the **Instagram Growth Metric**:

1. Click on your *Instagram profile*
2. Select the *option menu* available in the upper left corner
3. Select '**Insights**'
4. Find '*Overview*' and tap on the *number of your followers*
5. A new page will open and the first available graph will be the '**Growth Metric**'.

Post Insights (Impressions). Under each one of your Instagram posts, you will see Post Insights, where you can find information about the performance of your individual Instagram posts. There you can learn how people discovered your posts – from Post Impressions. Instagram Post Impressions are the number of times your post has been viewed over a specific period of time. You can use Instagram Post Impressions to get information on how your audience discovers your account or to examine the success of your hashtag strategy. These Impressions can come from:

- Home – your followers' feed;
- Profile – people who've visited your Instagram profile;
- Location – people who clicked on your post from the location tag you've added;
- Hashtags – people who have found your content from hashtags;
- Other - people who saved your post or shared it through DMs; people coming from outside of Instagram; people specifically visiting your profile from another post your Instagram name has been tagged.
- Explore page - where viral content lives

To get access to the **Post Insights (Impressions)**:

1. Click on your *Instagram profile*
2. Select the *post* you want to learn more about
3. Tap on '**View Insights**', which you will find right above the like button
4. Pull up/Slide up the *new window* which shows your likes, comments, DM shares, saves, profile visits and reach.
5. Below '**Discovery**', you will find '**Impressions**'.

Story Insights. Similar to Post Insights, you can use Story Insights to measure the performance of your Instagram stories. If Instagram stories are part of your Instagram strategy, you need to pay attention to the metrics the app offers to analyze interactions received from stories – Story Insights. They can be a great indicator of how engaging your followers are with your Instagram account.

To get access to the **Story Insights**:

1. Click on your *Instagram profile*
2. Select the *option menu* available in the upper left corner
3. Select '**Insights**'
4. Find '**Content You Shared**' and tap on '**Stories**'
5. Sort your recent stories based on Reach, Follows, Exits, Impressions, Link Clicks, etc.

With Story Insights, you can get access to analytics such as how many people visited your profile and reacted to your story. You can also use them to find out how many people have clicked or interacted with a sticker you've added or to track website links (Swipe up) you've received from the specific story. Last, but not least, you can find Insights about your story even if it is not available anymore (up to 30 days before the data disappears).

Post Engagement - Profile visits, Saves & DM shares. If you pay regular attention to how your latest Instagram posts are performing, you will soon get an idea of how many interactions you get on average in terms of likes, comments, follows, saves, and DM shares. This will give you an estimation of what to expect when you share a post. The more engaging content you share, the more profile visits, posts Saves, and DM share you will receive. Analyzing and monitoring these metrics can give your Instagram account an advantage – you will be able to determine if one post is going to get high engagement and have the viral element or not once the content is posted. The more people save it and share it through Instagram DMs, the better results you can expect.

To get access to the **Profile visit**:

1. Click on your *Instagram profile*
2. Select the *option menu* available in the upper left corner
3. Select '**Insights**'
4. Find '**Overview**' and tap on the number of account reached
5. Under '**Account Activity**', you will find '**Profile visits**'

To get access to **Saves and DMs**:

1. Click on your *Instagram profile*
2. Select the *post* you want to learn more about
3. Tap on '**View Insights**', which you will find right above the like button
4. Pull up/Slide up the *new window* where you can see your likes, comments, DM shares, saves, profile visits and reach.

Note: Unfortunately, Instagram recently removed DM shares from Post Insights for the European countries due to new laws.

CTA links. Call To Action (CTA) such as email and website links, as well as the get directions feature can reveal a lot about your content Marketing. Use these metrics to tailor your strategy by analyzing the type of content that brings best results outside of the platform.

If you want to take a step further, you can also keep an eye on each one of your strategy posts with the help of Post Insights. There, you can find out if someone visited your website or took the required action from the exact post. Pay attention to how your content is performing – which posts get the most traction.

To get access to **Call To Action (CTA)**:

1. Click on your *Instagram profile*
2. Select the *option menu* available in the upper left corner
3. Select '**Insights**'
4. Find '**Overview**' and tap on the number of account reached
5. Under '**Account Activity**', you will find '**Email Button Taps**' and '**Website Taps**'

To get access to **Call To Action (CTA)** data from a specific post:

1. Click on your *Instagram profile*
2. Select the *option menu* available in the upper left corner
3. Select '**Insights**'
4. Find '**Content You Shared**' and tap on '**Posts**'
5. Sort your recent posts based on Call Button Taps, Email Button Taps, Get Directions Taps, Text Button Taps or Website Taps

Best time to post. If you have a Professional account with at least 100 followers, there is a metric that will tell you the best time to post on the platform. Posting at the time when your followers are most active will help you get more interactions on your latest post which will increase your accounts' engagement rate and the chance of getting on the Explore page.

To get access to **Best time to post**:

1. Click on your *Instagram profile*
2. Select the *option menu* available in the upper left corner
3. Select '**Insights**'
4. Find '**Overview**' and tap on the number of your followers
5. Scroll until the end of the page, where you will find '**Most Active Times**' for every day of the week

Part 3: Utilize the right strategy - Additional Tools for businesses and influencers

If you find it hard to stay focused on your Instagram account, there are numerous online tools to help you grow your channel and find what you are looking for. These tools can be used to create better content and improve your Instagram account. From scheduling apps to editing and designing apps, here is a list with some of the best tools brands and personal profiles can use to improve their online presence.

Scheduling Tools

With the help of scheduling tools, you will forget about manual posting. Such apps allow users to prepare content in advance and share it at the most appropriate time for their audience.

- **Tailwind**. Tailwind is an official Instagram Partner and it is an excellent app to use if you want to schedule your content. It automatically chooses the best time to auto-post your content on Instagram. You can use the app to come up with a plan of how often you want to post on the platform. Tailwind offers many features including Hashtag Finder and the option to visually plan your Instagram feed.

- **Hootsuite**. Hootsuite is a Social Media management app that offers up to 30 scheduled posts per month for free. It has a simple design and it is relatively easy to use. You can use the app to monitor your Instagram feed and engage with your audience. Or you can also measure the performance of your Instagram posts.

- **Later**. Another excellent scheduling tool for Instagram content is Later. Similar to Tailwind, the app offers a visual planner which can help you get a better idea of what your Instagram feed will look like. You can use Later to analyze how your Instagram content is performing or to improve your Instagram Marketing strategy.

- **Buffer**. Buffer is a famous Social Media scheduler that allows users to schedule Instagram posts, analyze the performance of their posts and manage their Social Media channels. Except scheduling posts, the platform has a Hashtag Manager that helps you reach more people. Users can create, save and organize hashtags and experiment which set of hashtags work best with the help of Instagram analytics.

- **Planoly**. Another visual planner that I enjoy using is Planoly. The app offers 30 free uploads every month. You can create hashtags groups that you can easily add to your Instagram post; manage your Instagram feed and track the performance of your latest posts.

- **Sked**. With Sked, you can automatically publish your Instagram posts but this is not the only feature it offers. You can use the app to visually plan your content, add a shopping tag to your posts or to get deep Instagram analytics about your posts and stories.

Design Tools

There are many design tools that will help you create stunning Instagram visuals that will bring more followers, traffic and engagement to your Instagram page. Some of the best of them are:

- **Canva**. With Canva, you can create Instagram posts and stories in the form of videos and pictures. Canva offers ready-to-publish Instagram posts designed by professionals that you can easily use, download and share to Instagram. You can choose from thousands of pre-designed templates that you can use for free. In addition, the app also offers free stock photos that people can use.

- **Crello**. Crello is very similar to Canva. It gives users the opportunity to create high quality content in minutes. It is easy to use and you can choose from stock images and videos as well as different text fonts and animations.

- **Animaker**. Animaker is a great app to make engaging Instagram videos with little to no effort. Similar to the rest of the designing platforms, it offers pre-existing designs that users can use as foundation for their work.

- **Adobe Spark**. Adobe Sparks is a great free design program that you can use on your computer or phone to create awesome graphics for Instagram in just a few minutes. The app has many different images, type styles, color schemes, filters, themes and layouts that users can choose from to create Instagram posts and stories.

- **VSCO**. VSCO is a mobile photo and video editing app that will help you take your smartphone shots to another level. The app is famous for creating beautiful shots with the help of amazing photo filters.

- **Adobe Lightroom**. Another great and very powerful photo and camera editing app is Adobe Photoshop Lightroom. It is a free to use mobile app, very similar to the desktop version. It allows users to create incredible shots with the help of presets, photo adjusting options, filters and much more.

- **Creative Market**. On Creative Marketing, you can find over 9000 templates to elevate your Instagram posts and create awesome visuals. You can use one of their pre-designed graphics to create a cohesive, visually appealing Instagram feed.

Hashtag Tools

- **Sistrix**. One free to use digital tool that will help you discover a new Instagram hashtag is Sistrix. If you want to get started, simply enter your core (main) hashtags. Based on the hashtags you have selected, you will get the best 30 hashtags related to it.

- **Autohash**. Autohash is a free Android app that uses a computer algorithm to discover new hashtags for your Instagram posts. The app will provide you with relevant hashtags based on the object in your post.

Instagram Analytics Tools

If you are a beginner, I recommend you start with Instagram Insights. They will give you everything necessary to start growing your channel. If you would like to try another way to track the performance of your Instagram profile, consider using some of the apps listed below:

- **Social Insider**. Social Insider is a digital tool that will provide you with important information about your Instagram profile. You can use this app to learn more about your content, brand and campaign analytics with the help of key metrics that will track your engagement and reach.

- **IconoSquare**. IconoSquare offers advanced analytics to maximize your Social Media performance. You can use this tool to keep a close eye on your performance as well as to get insightful industry benchmarks. IconoSquare enables users to dig deep into the insights of their Instagram profile.

- **Keyhole**. Keyhole allows users to measure and track their Instagram ad campaigns and calculate their ROI (Return On Investment). It helps you tailor a better Instagram strategy and create top-performing content.

Bonus

Ghost followers

Have you ever heard of ghost followers on Instagram?

Ghost followers are not your typical follower. They are Instagram accounts that follow you but are inactive. They are not the same as bots. Instead, these accounts were once active but now they are abandoned. So, they don't like or engage with your content in any way. You can try to identify ghost followers by looking at the users who follow you. A common pattern for ghost followers are:

- Having 0 followers but following thousands
- Having no bio & profile picture
- Having an abnormal username, filled with random characters.
- Having no recent posts for the last 30/60/90 days.

Are ghost followers bad for your Instagram account?

Nobody likes having ghost followers but most of us have them. Ghost followers are abandoned Instagram accounts of people, who have tried to use the platform but for one reason or another do not use it anymore. The longer you have your Instagram account for, the bigger the chance of having ghost followers. It is natural. You can't control the actions of other people and how active they are. Think of it this way - the more followers you have, the more potential ghost followers you might get over time.

Unfortunately, having too many ghost followers can have a negative impact on your engagement rate. If some of these abandoned accounts are hacked and turned into fake followers, there is a very big chance that Instagram will remove them over a certain amount of time.

The rest of the ghost followers you can combat by bringing more active followers to your account. You can use a combination of the different methods described in Part 2 of this book and find which one brings you the most engagement.

Part 4: Monetize your profile

This chapter of the book will focus on how to monetize your Instagram profile as a brand or a personal profile. To earn money from Instagram, you don't need to have thousands of followers (unless you are a personal profile looking to collaborate with bigger brands). But you need to have a decent engagement rate and create high-quality content. If you have a small community of people who genuinely engage with your content and you are passionate about what you do, you will not find it hard to monetize your Instagram profile even if you have a couple of hundred followers. Having said that, let's take a look at how brands and personal profiles can make money on Instagram.

Before we continue with this part of the book, I want to address IGTV Ads. Instagram is currently testing a monetization program for those of you who use IGTV. The plan is to run ads in your IGTV video and get 55% of the resulting revenue. Sounds sweet but it is still not available to the mass users, so I might cover this topic later on.

In order to make it easier to read, I've divided this part of the book into two sections - how to monetize your Instagram profile as a brand and how to do it as a personal profile.

Part 4: Monetize your profile - Personal profiles

If you are an Influencer, writer, musician or any type of creator on Instagram, you will find the following monetization options very helpful.

Collaboration

We have already discussed how collaborating with fellow creators can help you grow your Instagram account. Now, it is time to focus on how to make money as a personal profile while collaborating.

Collaboration is when influencers/creators work with brands. It is one of the most widespread ways to make money on Instagram. It can be when a brand approaches you by offering you some kind of payment for posting a post of their product to your feed. Or it can be the other way around - you approach a brand with an interesting offer to promote some of their products to your Instagram audience.

Every collaboration has different terms and requirements. But it can be beneficial for both sides. The brand can show their product to a group of targeted people, which might be interested in making a purchase. While influencers and creators can earn money or get free products for simply posting on their Instagram feed. Plus, if the collaboration is successful, the brand might want to work with you again in the future or extend your partnership by making you a brand ambassador or offering you an affiliate program.

If your goal is to collaborate with brands, make sure their products or services match your Instagram audience. Don't collaborate with brands just because they are offering something to you. Quite the opposite, make sure your target audience will like the products you endorse. Promoting irrelevant products would not lead to any sales for the brand you are collaborating with, but it would also affect your profile as you can start losing followers.

How to start?

In order to collaborate with brands, you need to have good analytics. Having a solid foundation of followers on your Instagram account will give you more and better collaboration offers. But followers are not everything. You can still get offers to work with brands if you have a small community of followers but a decent engagement rate (likes and comments) on your Instagram posts. However, if you want to make a living out of Instagram, then you will need to have at least a couple of thousands of followers and genuine engagement. If you have these two, you can proceed with the Step-by-step on how to get your first collaboration.

Step 1: Get yourself a Media Kit

Before you approach a brand and start sending a crazy amount of emails, it would be a great idea to create a media kit. A media kit is a one-page document that has every necessary information that one company would need to know about your Instagram profile. It consists of your analytics - the number of your followers, and other relevant information such as statistics of how your account is performing in terms of Impressions and Reach, story views, etc. You can find this information on your phone - from the Instagram app (Insights) or computer - by visiting Facebook Creator Studio -> Instagram.

Note: To access your Instagram analytics, you will need to have a Professional Instagram account.

Once you have the required information, you can create your media kit from scratch or you can use online software like Canva to design and customize your document. When your media kit is ready, you can start making a list of potential companies you want to collaborate with.

Example of a Media Kit:

Step 2: Make a List

Finding a brand that is not connected to your target group can affect both sides, but mostly you. While a brand will lose a product or some of their advertising budget, you will lose followers that you don't want to be losing. Thus, you need to know your followers and their interests and preferences. This will help you collect a list of brands to work with. Plus, finding a relevant product to promote will gain the trust of your followers instead of losing them. Just be realistic. If you are a small account and this is your first collaboration, don't reach out to already huge brands - they might not even respond to your email. Instead, try to work with smaller brands and especially startups. While they won't pay that much, you will get the experience to work with brands and you will know what to expect from future collabs.

Step 3: The email

To find the email of the brand you want to contact, you will need to spend some time researching their contact information. You can start by checking their Social Media channels and especially LinkedIn profile. If you don't find it there, you can visit their website. Many companies add an email to their website "Contact us" page or "About us", so make sure to check there too. If nothing works, you can ask the brand for their contact information through Twitter or Facebook messages.

If you are the one reaching up to a brand, you need to make it count as they are probably extremely busy. The email you send the company should contain the following:

- Introduction. A quick introduction will get the brand to know about who are you and what you do

- Reason. Why did you pick this brand? Why do you love their products?

- Interest. Why are you interested in working with this brand?

- Call To Action. Once you are done with the email, a nice CTA can be a great reminder to get a reply from the brand.

- Attachment. Do not forget to add your Media Kit as an attachment to your email. This is how the brand will get a better understanding of your Instagram profile and audience.

The email should not be too long. You want to make it sound as sweet and catchy as possible, so a few sentences will do the work. Don't repeat the same thing over and over again, but also make sure your email is full of valuable information. Once you send the email, give the brand a few days (up to a week). If they don't answer (which but possible), write a follow-up email.

It might take time until you find a brand to work with, but when you do, you will feel so satisfied with your effort and how much you have learned. If a brand is interested in your proposal, they would want to hear more about it, so then and only then you can write a long email, describing your idea of this collaboration.

If you run out of patience and emails to contact, you can check out websites that connect influencers with a brand. A great example of that type of a website is Tomoson or the app Tribe. However, the chances of getting sponsorship through a middleman are not as big because there is a lot of competition and it is not as personal as writing an email.

If a brand reaches out to you

If a company wants to work with you, it means that your dream is coming true and people find you online. But that doesn't mean that you will accept it right away. When a brand contacts you, they will usually have an idea in mind. They will know what they want and what they are looking for. If you think that they will be a good fit for your account and your audience, working with them is advised. But if they are not a match for your audience, you should keep looking for a better collaboration.

Note: Remember to disclose your sponsored posts on Instagram. Use the hashtag #ad under your sponsored content and use the Instagram feature called 'Tag Business Partner'. This feature will tag your post with a label 'Paid partnership with' and the partner's name. You can find it in Advanced Settings, when creating a new post on Instagram.

You will need to disclose your sponsored posts if you have any US audience as the FTC law requires you to do so. If you think that this law won't apply to you, chances are that you are wrong because if you have at least one US viewer, this law applies to your profile too.

Affiliate programs

As a personal profile, you have a lot of opportunities to make money from your account. If collaborations are not for you because they take too much time or you get discouraged, there is something similar that you might want to try out - join an affiliate program.

Affiliate marketing is a relationship between a merchant and a personal profile, in which the merchant pays a commission to the personal profile for sending traffic via link to their site. Most of the time, the commission is paid only when an actual sale is made as a result from this link. To paraphrase, when you are an affiliate, you will make money by selling products. With the help of a trackable link, you will be able to keep a track of how many products you have sold and what is your commission.

Unlike collaborating with brands, affiliate programs are not a one-time offer. They are a long-term deal, where personal profiles get paid every time a sale is made. If you want to be successful in affiliate marketing on Instagram, it is important to start by finding a product you like and you can sell. You would want to sell something to your target group that they find relevant. After all, they are the one buying the products.

Before you pick the product/s you want to promote, browse and look for reviews and feedback that will point you whether the item is worth it. But, a general rule of thumb - do not sell products that you don't believe in, or you won't buy.

There are many ways to become an affiliate. To find an affiliate program, you can contact brands you like with a reasonable offer or you can browse on some of the most popular marketplaces for affiliates. The top three that are worth your attention are - Clickbank (payment - commission), RewardStyle (20% commission) and Amazon's Affiliate Program (10% commission).

Affiliate marketing requires a lot of creativity and it is not as simple as it looks. The biggest problem with affiliate programs is that you can add only one link to your Instagram profile. This limits the number of products you can promote. The best thing you can do in this situation is to add the affiliate link to your biography and try to add your promo code (if you have one) to the captions of your posts and encourage your audience to visit the link with strong CTAs. If your selected product is not selling, then you might need to freshen up your feed, look at the selection of hashtags you are using or create more interactive captions that will grab the attention of your followers. Instagram stories are also advised when it comes to promoting products, services and events.

Quick Tip: Nobody likes long URLs because they can be pretty annoying and look scammy. So, if your affiliate link is too long, you can use an online tool to shorten the URL and add it to your biography.

Open a shop

Collaborations and affiliate programs are great to get you started and show you that it is possible to make money from Instagram. But if you have more time to focus on your Instagram account, you can use it to build something yours - like to open an online shop.

The best thing about the Internet is that there are so many people, that you can literally sell anything. This works because Social Media is the best place to promote products, mainly because it is free and so many people use it. Not only that, but Instagram is the best place to promote your new business venture as it is the platform with the highest engagement.

You can sell your crafts or offer a service. If you are an artist, you can sell your paintings or create T-shirts and sell them. Or you can write a book and market it on Instagram. If you have access to an audience, interested in what you are selling, you can sell a lot and make just as much money. It is all about creativity and the art of selling. If you come up with something unique, detailed and interesting for the group of people following you, you can build yourself an empire. If you are able to establish a loyal audience of thousands of people, then you can earn a lot. This can be a game-changer for you.

Building an online shop can be so much easier when you have an audience that cares about you and listens to your opinion. So how to start?

In today's world, there is a platform for everything. So opening an online shop is no exception. You can create your own online shop on Shopify, Etsy, WooCommerce, etc. There are many choices to choose from, so it is up to you. When you set your website, add a list of products and change your URL by purchasing a domain name so you can remove shopify.com from your shop URL, you will be ready to start promoting your products on Instagram.

Opening your own shop as an established self-branded figure is easy. But doing it while you grow and manage your Instagram is not an easy task for everyone because some people are not ready to invest the time. Make sure you can handle the task before you move forward with your plans.

If you want to read more about selling online, you can go to Part 4: Monetize your profile - Brands: Sell online.

Sell pictures

If you have good photography equipment (preferably a DSLR) and a passion for photography, there are some ways to make money from Instagram by focusing on this exact talent. For example, if you are a photographer and use the geotag on your posts and Instagram stories frequently, there is a very high chance to get clients from Instagram. Or you can own a blog about what makes you good at photography, tips on how to improve and what type of editing tools to sing and monetize it once it gets enough viewers. But most importantly, you can also sell your photos. How?

Stock photos are huge these days. If you are a blogger, advertiser or have a website, chances are that you have used stock photos in your life and you know exactly how valuable and time-saving they can be. No wonder there are so many people willing to pay in order to get the best images for their business.

So, if you have the eye for a good picture, the equipment to create one and an Instagram gallery to use as a portfolio of your work, you have the possibility to earn hundreds, if not thousands of dollars. But before you get hyped about all the money you can make, you need to add your high-quality photos to a marketplace, where they can be sold. There are many platforms selling stock photos.

Here are some suggestions to get you started:

• Foap. This platform is a very successful one, so don't be afraid if there is a lot of competition with great shots. When you sell a photo, you earn $5. The best thing about it is that you can sell the same photo over and over again for an unlimited time. Plus, the platform offers contests, where a brand asks for a particular type of photo and the best image wins. It is called Missions. Usually, brands pay higher than $5, so this is another way to earn yourself some extra cash, which can sometimes be up to $500.

• Twenty20. Another great marketplace that operates very similar to Foap is Twenty20. The only difference is that you make $2 per photo that you sell. You can also enter challenges and get commissions when you work with brands.

   • Lobster.Media. The platform allows you to keep 75% of the price you have listed. Selling on Lobster.Media can be great and easy, as long as you put a normal, realistic price.

Once you have found the right marketplace for your pictures, you can start promoting the best of your work on Instagram. This is very similar to selling a product, but in this case, you are selling your own art - your pictures. Remember to add the link that leads to your portfolio to your Instagram biography.

Quick Tip: The more natural the picture looks, the bigger chances for success you have. Plus, photography is a talent with a little bit of editing skills required. So, don't force the great shot, let it happen and compliment it with the right combination of Brightness, Highlights, Shadow, Exposure and Contrast.

Sell shoutouts

If you know other accounts in your niche, who have the same passion for your topic, all of you can earn money by working together. You can build a new Instagram account for shoutouts.

To do so, you will need to prepare content in advance. You can curate content from your niche, post it and give credits to the owner of the post. The more you grow your account, the more attractive it gets. Also, you can create a branded hashtag that people from your niche can use in order to have a chance to get featured on your Instagram page. But you need to find time to invest in growing your account by engaging with other relevant accounts.

The idea of having more people moderating the same account will help you to manage and grow it easier. To be even more efficient, you can give your new Instagram shoutout account a lot of exposure by making each one of the moderators promote it on their own profile. Of course, you can run the account alone but you will have to do everything yourself. This sounds like a lot of work considering that you have your own account to manage as well.

Shoutouts can be super effective for new accounts but also for the already established profiles. So, there is no wonder that you can also make money out of it. But you will have to walk a long way before you get there. That being said, making money from shoutouts is not hard, but it takes time to grow the account. To successfully monetize your account you will need to have at least 100 000 followers and good engagement. A lot of likes and a variety of comments will give you the option to increase the amount you charge per post.

Not every shoutout is successful. Some of them won't bring you even one like or profile visit. So, you will need to work hard to win the trust of your audience and make sure your audience will engage with the content you share. If your Instagram shoutout account has a very engaging community and people are getting results from your shoutouts, you can get a lot of requests.

Shoutout account suggestions can be anything related to your niche. For example, if you have an Instagram account of your dog, you can create a shoutout account for dog features.

Part 4: Monetize your profile - Brands

This part of the book will focus on how to make money on Instagram as a brand. Whether you are in the B2C or B2B market, your goal should always be to earn more money by promoting your products or services to increase sales and find new clients/customers.

So, how to make money as a brand on Instagram?

Sell Online

A lot of online shops fail to drive sales through Instagram and quit shortly after because most of them don't have a group of followers willing to buy their products. Often, they use follow/unfollow and other harmful ways to make their profile look more appealing to potential customers who just discovered their profile through an ad or some other way. But Social Media is not about selling, it is about socializing. Forming your own community of people with similar interests to whom you can sell to.

Having an engaging audience can make your brand look more trustworthy. Many eCommerce businesses do not understand the importance of building a reputable and trustworthy brand. But lack of trust and good customer experience can have a huge impact on your sales. It is extremely hard to sell a product without making people trust your brand and believe in your message. But building trust takes time. It is much harder than staying active and posting content but connecting with your audience in any way possible. Excellent customer service and replying to comments and DMs is a great start if you are a new brand.

Whether you are starting just now or you are an established company, Instagram highlights can be another great addition to your page. You can use them to provide more detailed information about your company. Something people would want to know about such as FAQ, About Us, Customer Reviews, Blog, etc.

Create great content but don't be too pushy about selling your products. Instead, try to mix up your feed with content that would make your audience more engaging - quotes, entertaining posts, etc and company posts - products, company info, upcoming events, etc. Use your common interest to provide value before you push your products. Here are some content ideas you might find interesting:

Tell a story. People love a good story. Creating a compelling story will make your account more trustworthy and relevant for your target group.

Use videos. Posting videos on Instagram can go either bad or very good. But if you make a good video, your account will get more engagement and views than most of your photos. So, before you pick a video, make sure that it is good for your target audience, it is high-quality and there are no side noises. I have noticed that videos with high engagement stay longer on the Explore page - you can still get likes, comments, and followers from them even one week after they have been posted.

Post emotional content. People buy based on emotion. Most of the purchases are bought because of the emotional message behind them. It can be because of greed - maybe to save money, because of fear of missing out or because of love, you want to make someone happy. And that's exactly what you need to do with your Instagram posts as a brand - you want to convince the emotional side of your followers that they need to own your product. Think about what emotional buttons you can trigger with your posts.

Entertain your followers with funny pictures. Who doesn't love to laugh?

Your content can help your followers to get through a bad day. This will make them more attached to your profile.

Post inspirational quote. Similar to laughter, motivation can go a long way. Some try to escape from negative emotions such as anger, boredom, sadness through Social Media. So, seeing an inspirational quote can make/fix their day because sometimes all of us need a little push or something to give us motivation.

Offer value to your followers. Whether you are a product store and you are offering a discount code through your post or you are posting informative pictures/videos for a particular niche, giving something for free might increase the number of your followers and make your current audience more attached to your account. In addition, offering a special offer or value will give you credibility.

Ask questions. Posts with questions get more engagement than the one with a simple caption because when you ask your followers for an opinion you are encouraging them to share it with you. Plus, engaging with the comments will show them that you care and you are interested to know the answer. So, a way to make your content more engaging is if you ask questions related to your target group.

Use trending events. As mentioned before, posting about trending events can help your account to get more exposure. However, this is true only when you can connect it to your niche. If this is not the case and there is no way you can spin it in your favour, then it might be good to don't participate and wait for another event that you can join. For example, events like Valentine's Day and Christmas are the ones relatively easy to post about. But if Mother's Day is approaching and your brand has nothing to do with this day, the best thing you can do is to skip the event and move on.

Act like a professional. You will need to make your profile strong and don't let people know your flaws. Even if it is a mess behind the scenes, you need to act like a professional. That doesn't mean that you have to lie to your followers - NOT AT ALL. Just be selective with your posts. Nobody is perfect and we all have ups and downs, but posting about your down moments won't leave a good name for you.

Make your posts shoppable. Instagram has made its platform shoppable. This means that users no longer need to leave Instagram in order to shop. Shoppable posts are a very powerful tool that brands can use in order to increase their sales. More and more countries have this feature and if you are lucky, so do you.

If you want to make your posts shoppable on Instagram and this option is available in your country, here is what you need to connect your Facebook shop to your Instagram account:

To do so, start the Instagram app, click on your profile and select 'Settings'. Then, you will have to navigate to "Business", where you will see "Sign Up for Shopping". If you don't see it, then either your country is not on the list and you can't use this feature or your account is under review. If you are seeing it, click in it, then press "Continue" and select the product catalog you want to connect to your Instagram. Tap "Done". That is it!

If your Facebook shop is empty, you can create a product catalog. You have to go to your Facebook page and click on "Shop". This will give you the opportunity to add products to your Facebook page. Once you fill the required fields with Name, Price, Description and Checkout URL (the link to the specific product), you have to click on "Save". When you have every product you want to tag on your Facebook page, you can go to your Instagram account. After that, when you try to create a new post, you will see "Tag Products". From there you will see all of the products from your Facebook page. When you find the product that you have featured in this post, just select it and tap on the picture to place the tag.

Note: If you tag products, you cannot tag people.

This feature can be very beneficial for your business. The only last thing for you to do is earn money. If you have an already built audience, this won't be hard, not at all.

If you already use Instagram Shopping, you will love this news – Instagram is testing a new feature called IGTV Shopping. What does it mean for your business?

With IGTV Shopping, businesses have the option to tag products from their

Facebook catalogue/Shop in their IGTV video. This new feature allows companies to increase their sales without spending a cent advertising. If Instagram users want to purchase from your IGTV video, they can do it via Instagram Checkout or through your website.

At the moment, Instagram accounts who have access to Instagram Checkout have the option to use IGTV Shopping on their channel. Instagram Checkout is a new feature that enables users to buy products directly from the app. It is only available to U.S. businesses and creators because it is still in beta.

Influencer Marketing

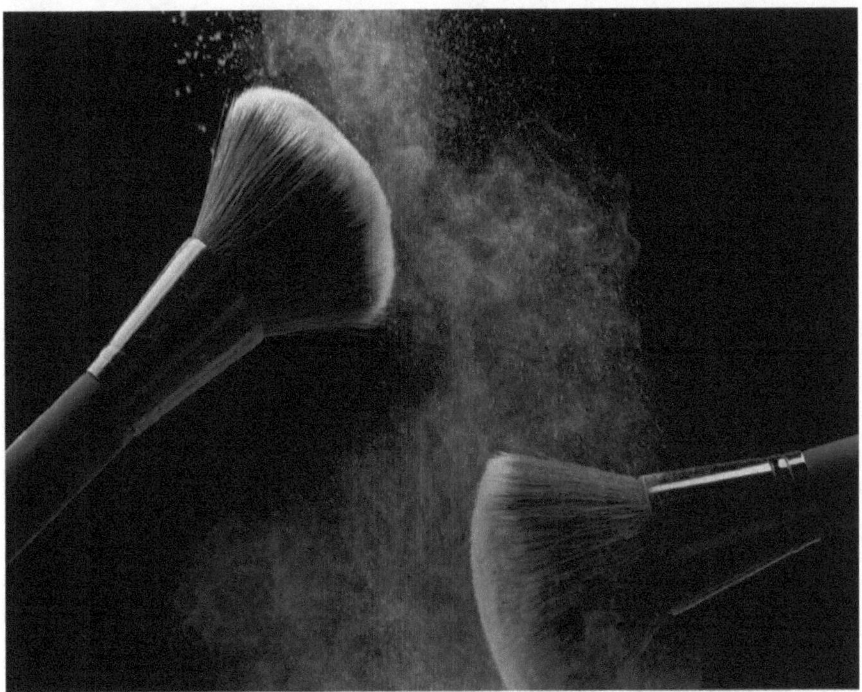

Influencer Marketing (IM) is a form of collaboration between brands and influencers (personal profiles). It is when brands work with influential people with an effort to promote their products or services. Within any industry, there are influential people. These are the people with a large following and online influence. Such people can be celebrities but also any content creator who has a niche and engaging audience on their Instagram profile. Content creators that have spent time building their own audience had the patience to grow organically.

Influencer Marketing is a very powerful marketing tool you can use to build credibility online, increase your brand's awareness and sales. But in order to run a successful IM campaign, you will need to find the right influencer.

The right influencer

Choosing the right influencer to work with can be very time-consuming. You need to pick someone that works well with your business and matches your target group. Someone who has an audience you can describe as the "perfect customer" for your business. In order to do that, you will need to determine the type of influencer you want to promote your products/services. If you are certain Instagram is the best platform to reach your audience, you can choose between micro- and celebrity influencers.

Celebrity influencers. These are the people with a large following (millions) who are widely recognized across many industries. They have a huge number of followers and more influence over them. Although having a huge audience sounds tempting, it is important to choose your influencer carefully. Celebrities endorsement is not cheap but it can be great for brands, looking to increase their brand awareness and provide social proof. But it is not so great for the ones looking to reach a specific niche of people.

Micro-Influencers. Unlike celebrity influencers, micro-influencers have a relatively small group of followers but they specify in one niche. This number can vary between a couple of thousands and tens of thousands of followers within their niche. Having a smaller audience allows them to engage and build a relationship with the group of people who follow them more regularly. They create high-quality content and the engagement rate of their account is high. Because of this, they are great to work with brands, looking to form personal relationships among their group of followers and increase the number of their sales.

Quick Tip: Pay attention to their engagement rate. A higher engagement rate will indicate that their followers are real and not bought. Make sure to look at the people that comment under their pictures – are they unique or they are the same exact people every time. If that's the case, chances are that the influencer is part of a POD. So, take enough time to analyze their account to avoid getting scammed from fake influencers, looking for free products or payments.

Quick Tip 2: If you are unsure about their engagement, take a step further and find a website that will point to how many of their followers are fake. Most of the time, this is very obvious. For example, it is IMPOSSIBLE for an account with 40 000 followers to get merely 300 likes. It just doesn't work that way. An acceptable number for such an account is at least 1000 likes.

You need to determine which one is the best option for your business and the objective you want to achieve with this promotion. This will be an important step for determining your campaign budget. Whatever you decide, you need to look out for influencers, who have similar to your Instagram feed, style, aesthetics, and personal touch.

Strategy

Influencer Marketing can be effective only by executing the right strategy and tools. When planning a strategy, there are a few things to take into consideration:

1. Your company's goals
2. Target audience
3. Campaign budget

Company's goals

Before you use Influencer Marketing, it is very important to understand why you need it for your business. It can be for one of these reasons - for social proof and brand awareness or to convert more sales and attract more of your target audience. Either way, it is crucial to know the objective you are going for before you start reaching out to influencers. This will help you identify the audience you want to reach. Celebrity influencers can help with brand awareness, while micro-influencers can promote your product to a very niche audience and increase your sales.

Once you know the type of influencer you are looking for, you can focus on determining the structure and company message behind your campaign. Choose a message that aligns with your campaign goal. Be specific about what you want and make sure to prepare guidelines for the influencer/s you work with. There, you can include important brand details such as your brand voice, style, what to do / what not to do. While you do all of this, make sure to give the influencer some creative control as well.

Quick Tip: Make sure to check and approve the posts before the influencer uploads them because they are representing your brand.

Target audience

Before you set up your campaign, make sure you are familiar with your target audience. Identifying your ideal customer can help you find the best influencer whose audience is the perfect match for your business. This can turn into a very successful collaboration.

However, if you don't spend enough time researching your target group and identifying the ideal customer for your business, the results won't be satisfying. If your brand offers a product to a group of uninterested people, you will lose money and time.

Campaign budget

If you know the objective you want to achieve and the audience you want to reach, it is time to set the budget for your Influencer Marketing campaign. Consider your campaign budget very carefully and make sure it is profitable for your business. Choose the best payment option for your influencer campaign. If you want a bigger campaign, consider including more than one influencer. Make sure all of them are on the same page with the message you want to send. Then, select a payment option that aligns with the goals of your campaign:

Money payment. If you choose this option for your IM campaign, the influencer will receive money prior to or after the content is uploaded, depending on your agreement. The larger the audience of one influencer, the more they can charge your brand. So, make sure your company can afford it. If you are a startup and do not have the money to pay influencers, consider working with micro-influencers. If your company has more resources, you might choose to work with a celebrity influencer as you have the option to spend more money.

Brand ambassador. The brand ambassador program is very similar to affiliate marketing but ambassadors do not receive a commission when one product is sold. With this option, the influencer can receive product samples such as makeup, clothes, accessories from your brand or an up-front fee, depending on your agreement. The brand ambassador program is the perfect solution to put a human face on your brand. This will make your brand more personal and people will connect with you much easier than before. It is best to choose people who would love to represent your brand because they genuinely like and believe in your products. Otherwise, if the ambassador is not a good fit, it might not be worth the expense.

Affiliate Marketing. This option is very popular for eCommerce businesses looking to increase their sales. With affiliate marketing, the influencer will receive a commission for every sale of your products made by their audience. Companies who offer affiliate programs, use trackable links to determine how much one influencer has sold. So, influencers will make money, only when they sell from their link or promo code. Recruiting affiliates can be very time-consuming but if successful, it can bring your company great results. If you don't know how to make your own affiliate campaign, there are plenty of online websites that connect brands to influencers.

Whatever payment option you choose, make sure it is reasonable for both - your company and the influencer. Once you have your company's goals, target audience, and budget, it is time to find the right influencer to promote your products/services.

How to find the right influencer?

There are many ways to find influencers. If you are looking for a micro-influencer, Social Media can be an excellent place to start. You can search for specific keywords and use hashtags on Instagram in order to find the people with the most influential and engaging posts in a specific niche. Or you can use third-party software that connects businesses and already proven influencers in all sorts of categories and industries. Popular platforms are Upfluence, Tapinfluence, Tribe, and Hypetap.

If you are looking to hire a celebrity influencer, this process is a little bit more complicated. You will have to go through a talent agency or an agent to determine if a celebrity is willing to work with you and for what budget.

Before you reach out to an influencer, make sure to analyze their profile and learn more about what they do. When you find the perfect match for your profile, make sure to answer yourself the following questions:

- ➤ What is their engagement rate?
- ➤ Do they have a consistent audience?
- ➤ Who is their target audience?
- ➤ How many people will the campaign reach approximately (based on their analytics that you can ask for)?
- ➤ Do they fit your brand image?
- ➤ Have they worked with anyone else from your niche?
- ➤ Do they collaborate with brands often?
- ➤ How frequently do they post?

Next, you would want to find the contact information of the influencer you want to work with. The best approach is through email. If you cannot find their email on Instagram, try other Social Media channels. When exchanging emails with influencers, remember to include details like:

- Your campaign plan - budget and message.
- Special requirements regarding the post/posts. Do you have anything that the influencer must include in the post?
- How many posts do you want the influencer to do? Usually, a brand will require 1-2 posts, but it is all up to you. Just make it reasonable for the payment you are offering.
- When will the payment be completed? After or before the post. Is it halfway now and halfway after the post or are you going to send a free product?
- If you are paying with a free sample of your products, then you need to ask for contact details.

If the influencer is a micro-influencer you can also try to reach them on Instagram through DMs. However, this is not the best option considering the Instagram Creator account will put your message in requests and it might never be seen.

Monitor your IM strategy

Just like anything else on Social Media, you will need to measure your campaign results once the Influencer campaign is active. This will determine how successful the campaign is in reaching your target audience.

If you use Google Analytics for your website, you will be able to track your overall traffic coming from Social Media, and especially Instagram.

If you ask the influencer to conduct a giveaway or content by tagging a branded hashtag for your campaign, pay attention to the people who participate in the campaign.

If you use affiliate programs, make sure to track the specific URLs you've given the influencer to estimate how many people visited the specific link.

If you want to measure the performance of the influencer's post, you can find online tools such as BuzzSumo, HubSpot's Social Tool, and BuzzStream. All of them have analytics tools that will help you determine the ROI from your Influencer Marketing campaign.

Quick Tip: If you are unhappy with the results of your campaign, try Instagram advertising.

Working with influencers is an opportunity provided by Social Media, especially Instagram. Brands love it because they can reach different audiences, with already established patterns and interests. Influencers love it because it gives them the opportunity to make a living by creating content. With Influencer Marketing, you can find the rhythm that works best for your brand and give a head start to your company.

Direct Messages (DMs)

Instagram Direct Messages (DMs) can be used by businesses in order to achieve different objectives. For companies in the business-to-business market, DMs can be used in order to reach out to potential clients. While brands who serve the business-to-customer sector can use them to expand their community of loyal customers, provide excellent customer service and increase sales.

DMs are great because they create a personal touch, allowing brands to connect with their customers on a more personal and more individual level. Similar to regular messages, you can use them to send text, picture or upload a video to a single person or form a group of up to 15 participants.

You can use DMs as part of your Instagram strategy:

To build relationships. DMs can be a great way to communicate with your audience as a brand. You can use Instagram Direct Messages to build and create relationships with your most devoted followers. This is an important step for businesses that want to form a community on Instagram because it allows them to connect with current and potential customers.

To share exclusive offers to your customers. With Instagram DMs, you can reward your loyal customers by sending them exclusive coupons and deals. This is a unique opportunity that allows brands to connect with customers in a unique and more personal way. You can use DMs to send a message about an upcoming sale or a new product.

To provide excellent customer service. With the help of Direct Messages and the feature Quick Reply (more information about this feature - Part 1: Time, Frequency & Analytics), brands can handle customer service issues better than before. Providing good customer service is extremely important and if handled poorly, it can result in a loss for your business.

To hold contests. Contests are great and your creativity is the limit. They can be a very powerful tool for your page and business. Contests get a lot of likes, comments, and actions, which boosts the engagement rate on your account. You can use DMs to run a contest. For example, you can create content in the form of posts and stories, asking people to send you a private message in order to enter the contest.

To find content. Whenever your customers tag your products on their stories, you will get a DM notification with the post in the first 24h before it disappears. So, you can use DMs to discover user-generated content. This type of content is extremely important if you want to have a trustworthy brand. User-generated content can help you build trust among your followers because the message comes directly from a peer rather than from your brand.

To reach out to potential clients. If you know your target audience is on Instagram, you can use DMs instead of cold calls and cold emails to find more clients for your business. This option is worth the try because unlike emails, you get a fast response from the potential client and unlike phone calls, you can ask for feedback if they say no to your proposal. You can use DMs to identify what works and what doesn't. Use them smart because if you send too many in a short period of time, you might get restricted or even worse.

Note: Do not send more than 20 and 100 DMs per day.